The Great Regression

The Great Regression

Edited by Heinrich Geiselberger

polity

First published in German as *Die große Regression. Eine internationale Debatte über die geistige Situation der Zeit* © Suhrkamp Verlag, Berlin, 2017

Preface © Heinrich Geiselberger, 2017, Ch.1 © Arjun Appadurai, 2017, Ch.2 © Zygmunt Bauman, 2017, Ch.3 © Donatella della Porta, 2017, Ch.4 © Nancy Fraser, 2017, Ch.5 © Eva Illouz, 2017, Ch.6 © Ivan Krastev, 2017, Ch.7 © Bruno Latour, 2017, Ch.8 © Paul Mason, 2017, Ch.9 © Pankaj Mishra, 2017, Ch.10 © Robert Misik, 2017, Ch.11 © Oliver Nachtwey, 2017, Ch.12 © César Rendueles, 2017, Ch.13 © Wolfgang Streeck, 2017, Ch.14 © David Van Reybrouck, 2017, Ch.15 © Slavoj Žižek, 2017

English translations of the Preface and Chapters 7, 10, 11, 12, 13 © Polity Press, 2017

Polity Press
65 Bridge Street
Cambridge CB2 1UR, UK

Polity Press
350 Main Street
Malden, MA 02148, USA

ISBN-13: 978-1-5095-2235-4
ISBN-13: 978-1-5095-2236-1 (pb)

A catalogue record for this book is available from the British Library.

Typeset in 10.5 on 12 pt Sabon by Toppan Best-set Premedia Limited
Printed and bound in Great Britain by Clays Ltd, St Ives PLC

The publisher has used its best endeavours to ensure that the URLs for external websites referred to in this book are correct and active at the time of going to press. However, the publisher has no responsibility for the websites and can make no guarantee that a site will remain live or that the content is or will remain appropriate.

Every effort has been made to trace all copyright holders, but if any have been inadvertently overlooked the publisher will be pleased to include any necessary credits in any subsequent reprint or edition.

For further information on Polity, visit our website: politybooks.com

Contents

Contributors

Arjun Appadurai, born 1949 in Mumbai, is Goddard Professor of Media, Culture and Communication at New York University and Visiting Professor at the Institute for European Ethnology at the Humboldt University, Berlin (2016/17).

Zygmunt Bauman, born 1925 in Posen, died 2017 in Leeds, taught latterly at the University of Leeds. He received many accolades for his work, including the Theodor W. Adorno Award (1998) and the Prince of Asturias Award (2013).

Donatella della Porta, born 1956 in Catania, is Professor of Political Science and Director of the Centre of Social Movement Studies at the Scuola Normale Superiore in Florence.

Nancy Fraser, born 1947 in Baltimore, is Henry A. and Louise Loeb Professor of Political and Social Science and Professor of Philosophy at the New School in New York.

Heinrich Geiselberger, born 1977 in Waiblingen, has been an editor at Suhrkamp Verlag since 2006.

Eva Illouz, born 1961 in Fès, is Professor of Sociology at the Hebrew University of Jerusalem and at the EHESS in Paris. She writes regularly for the Israeli daily newspaper *Haaretz*.

Ivan Krastev, born 1965 in Lukovit, is Chairman of the Centre for Liberal Strategies in Sofia and Permanent Fellow at the Institute of Human Sciences in Vienna. Since 2015, he has been a regular contributor to the *New York Times International Edition.*

Bruno Latour, born 1947 in Beaune, is Professor at Sciences Po Paris and at the Centre de sociologie des organisations. He has received multiple awards, including the 2013 Holberg Prize.

Paul Mason, born 1960 in Leigh, is an English author and award-winning television journalist. He worked for many years for the BBC and Channel 4 News and now writes regularly for the *Guardian.*

Pankaj Mishra, born 1969 in Jhansi, is an Indian essayist, literary critic and author. Amongst other publications, he writes for the *New York Times,* the *New York Review of Books* and the *Guardian.* In 2014 he received the Leipzig Book Award for European Understanding.

Robert Misik, born 1966 in Vienna, is a journalist and political writer. He writes for the daily newspaper *die tageszeitung* as well as the magazines *Falter* and *Profil* and manages the video blog 'FS Misik' on the website of the daily newspaper *Der Standard.* In 2009 he received the Austrian State Prize for Cultural Communication.

Oliver Nachtwey, born 1975 in Unna, is a sociologist at the Technische Universität Darmstadt whose research focuses on labour, inequality, protest and democracy. He writes regularly for daily and weekly newspapers and web portals.

César Rendueles, born 1975 in Girona, teaches sociology at the Universidad Complutense de Madrid.

Wolfgang Streeck, born 1946 in Lengerich, is a sociologist. From 1995 to 2014 he was Director of the Max Planck Institute for the Study of Societies in Cologne. His research centres on comparative political economy and theories of institutional change. He is a regular contributor to the *New Left Review*.

David Van Reybrouck, born 1971 in Bruges, is a writer, dramatist, journalist, archaeologist and historian. In 2011 he founded G1000, an initiative that campaigns for democratic innovations in Belgium, the Netherlands and Spain. His book *Congo: The Epic History of a People* received several awards, including the ECI Literature Prize, the NDR Kultur Nonfiction Prize and the Prix Médicis essai (all 2012). His articles appear in newspapers internationally, such as *Le Monde*, *La Repubblica* and *De Standaard*.

Slavoj Žižek, born 1949 in Ljubljana, teaches at the European Graduate School, Birkbeck, University of London, and at the Institute for Sociology at the University of Ljubljana.

Preface

Heinrich Geiselberger

> When a world order breaks down,
> that is when people begin to think about it.
> Ulrich Beck 2011[1]

The idea for this book arose in late autumn 2015, after a series of terrorist attacks had shaken Paris and as the debate in Germany about the arrival of hundreds of thousands of refugees became increasingly fraught. The reaction to these events in politics, the media and general discourse gave the impression that the world was suddenly falling below the standards it had fought hard to achieve and had thought of as secure.

Directly associated with terrorism and migration is the fact that all around the globe the number of territories in which a state as such no longer exists is growing. Syria, Afghanistan and Iraq, the three countries from which most people seeking asylum in Germany came in 2016, ranked near the top of the 'Fragile State Index' compiled by the NGO Fund for Peace in the same year.[2] While the blank spaces on the maps had grown smaller and smaller over the centuries, things now appear to be going in the opposite direction. In the age of Google Maps there are a growing number of territories of which one knows very little and which ancient cartographers would have marked with the phrase *hic sunt leones*. Furthermore, many of the political reactions to the terrorist attacks and the migrant wave fit the pattern of post-democratic gesture politics and what sociologists call 'securitization'. There are the calls for walls, and there has even been talk of orders to shoot at refugees trying to cross frontiers. The president of France has declared a state of emergency, saying that the country is at war. Unable to tackle the global causes of such challenges as immigration and terrorism or growing inequality at the national level, or to combat them with long-term strategies, more and more politicians rely on law and order at home, together with the promise to make their respective countries 'great again'.[3] In the Age of Austerity, it is evidently no longer possible to offer citizens much in their roles as workers, fellow sovereign citizens, school children or users of public infrastructure. In consequence, the political emphasis has shifted to the dimension of nationality, the promise of safety, and the restoration of the glory of a bygone age.

The list of the symptoms of decline could be extended almost indefinitely. We could highlight the yearning for an anarchic, unilateral de-globalization or the emergence of the Identitarian movement, as for example in France, Italy and Austria; or the growing xenophobia and Islamophobia, the wave of so-called hate crimes, and of course the rise of authoritarian demagogues such as Rodrigo Duterte, Recep Tayyip Erdoğan or Narendra Modi.

By the late autumn of 2015 all this was accompanied by an increased hysteria and a coarsening of public discourse, together with a certain herd mentality on the part of the established media. Evidently, people could no longer talk about flight and migration without invoking the semantic fields of 'natural catastrophes' and 'epidemics'. Instead of issuing calls for calm and pragmatism or contextualizing events historically and thus helping to see them in perspective, the risks of terrorism and immigration in Germany were turned into the greatest challenge not just since Reunification but even since the Second World War. At demonstrations as well as on the internet, terms such as 'lying press', 'dictatorship of the chancellor' and 'traitors to the people' (*Volksverräter*) instead of 'representatives of the people' (*Volksvertreter*) became common currency.

Symptoms such as these are discussed in the present book under the heading of 'the great regression'. Beyond the naive belief in progress that might be implicit in that term, it is intended to make clear that the ratchet effects of modernization appear to have lost their force in the most diverse spheres of activity and that we are witnessing a reversion to an earlier stage of 'civilized conduct'.[4] However, the term is intended also to point to a further puzzling phenomenon, namely that in the debates about the impact of globalization we have in some respects fallen back beneath the level that had already been reached almost twenty years ago. Two warnings that seem prophetic today were repeatedly recalled in the immediate aftermath of Donald Trump's victory. One was Ralf Dahrendorf's statement that the twenty-first century might well become the 'century of authoritarianism'.[5] The other was Richard Rorty's book *Achieving our Country*, in which the author analyses the effects of globalization (and the role of the 'cultural left') and lists a whole series of possible retrograde steps. He refers in particular to the rise of 'scurrilous demagogues', the growth of social and economic inequality, the onset of 'an Orwellian world', a rebellion of the people who have been left behind, and a return of 'sadism', resentment and disparaging remarks about women and ethnic minorities.[6]

The collection containing Dahrendorf's essay appeared in 1998, thus at the high point of the first wave of reflection about globalization. If we glance at the books of those years, we come across further statements that can be read as commentaries on the events of 2016. The German sociologist Wilhelm Heitmeyer warned against an 'authoritarian capitalism', 'repressive state politics' and 'rabid right-wing populism'.[7] Dani Rodrik prophesied that globalization would lead to 'social disintegration' and cautioned that a 'protectionist backlash' was not an unrealistic scenario.[8]

Many of the relevant assessments are based on something like a Polanyian mechanism of a Second Great Transformation. The Austro-Hungarian economic historian Karl Polanyi showed in his classic work *The Great Transformation*, which appeared in 1944, how the capitalist industrial society of the nineteenth century emerged out of smaller, feudal, agrarian conditions – politically, culturally and institutionally integrated – into something that led to a series of side effects and counter-movements until the economy was embedded once again at the level of national welfare states.[9] This phenomenon of both geographical and social expansion is repeating itself today at a moment when capitalism is leaving the boundaries of the nation-state behind it, and when, once again, it is accompanied by all sorts of side effects and counter-movements.[10] We need think only of the founding of Attac in 1998, the so-called 'Battle of Seattle' in 1999, and the first meeting of the World Social Forum in Porto Alegre in 2001 on the political left;[11] alternatively, of the first successes of anti-globalization populists on the political right: Pat Buchanan's surprisingly strong showing in the Republican primaries in 1996 (to which Rorty and Rodrik allude), or the success of Jörg Haider's FPÖ, which became the second-largest parliamentary party in Austria in the 1998 elections.

If we summarize the solutions put forward at the time, what was called for – echoing the movement described by Polanyi – was the re-embedding at the global level of an economy that had been let off the leash: by building transnational institutions, politics must be enabled to seek global solutions to global problems. Parallel to that, a corresponding mental attitude should emerge, a feeling of a cosmopolitan collective identity or 'we-feeling'.[12]

The bitter irony of this is that in the following years all the risks of globalization that were discerned at the time actually became reality – international terrorism, climate change, financial and currency crises, and lastly, great movements of migrants – while politically no one was prepared for them. Subjectively, there is evidently an utter failure to establish a robust sense of a cosmopolitan collective identity. On the contrary, we are at present witnessing a resurgence of ethnic, national and religious us/them distinctions. The logic of a 'clash of civilizations' has replaced the friend/foe pattern of the Cold War with astonishing speed, despite the supposed 'end of history'.

Against this background, after the expanding regression in late autumn 2015, the events that followed gradually combined to form a bleak panorama. These events included the conflict in Syria, the result of the Brexit referendum, the terrorist attack in Nice, the successes of the Alternative für

Deutschland (AfD) in Germany, the attempted coup in Turkey and the political reactions to it, and, finally, Trump's victory.

Whereas others had previously spoken of the *risks of globalization* in general, many of the writers in this volume stress that we are faced with a *neoliberal* version of globalization, so that we might with equal justice speak of the *risks of neoliberalism*. In this sense, the contributions collected here can be read as attempts to explore the question of the many different ways in which neoliberal democracies live on the basis of preconditions that they cannot themselves guarantee – to vary a phrase of Ernst-Wolfgang Böckenförde's.[13] These preconditions include media that provide a certain plurality of opinions; intermediate bodies such as trade unions, parties or associations in which people can achieve something like agency; genuine left-wing parties that succeed in articulating the interests of different milieus; and an education system that is not reduced to the production of 'human capital' and learning PISA tasks by heart.

The Great Regression that we are witnessing currently may be the product of a *collaboration* between the risks of globalization and neoliberalism. The problems that have arisen from the failure of politicians to exercise some control over global interdependence are impinging on societies that are institutionally and culturally unprepared for them.

This book sets out to pick up the threads of the globalization debate of the 1990s and to take it forward. In it, scholars and public intellectuals respond to urgent questions: How have we ended up in this situation? Where will we be in five, ten or twenty years' time? How can we stop the global regression and achieve a turnaround? In the face of an international league of nationalists the book attempts to create something like a transnational public sphere. The term 'transnational' here operates at three levels: first, that of the contributors; second, that of the phenomena under discussion; and third, that of distribution – the volume will appear simultaneously in several countries.

My thanks go first to the contributors for their willingness to take part in this venture and to produce substantial texts in a relatively short space of time. Thanks also to our international partner publishing houses for their belief in the project, and in particular to Mark Greif and John Thompson for their advice. This volume is also a project that would not have been possible without the assistance of my colleagues at Suhrkamp. A special word of thanks is due therefore to Edith Baller, Felix Dahm, Andrea Engel, Eva Gilmer, Petra Hardt, Christoph Hassenzahl, Christian Heilbronn, Nora Mercurio and Janika Rüter.

Berlin, December 2016
Translated by Rodney Livingstone

Notes

1 Ulrich Beck, 'Kooperieren oder scheitern. Die Existenzkrise der Europäischen Union', *Blätter für deutsche und internationale Politik*, 2 (2011), pp. 41–53.
2 J. J. Messner, *Fragile State Index 2016*, Washington, DC: Fund for Peace, 2016, p. 7.
3 Zygmunt Bauman, *Strangers at Our Door*, Cambridge: Polity Press, 2016.
4 On this point and on the concept of 'regressive modernization', see Oliver Nachtwey, *Die Abstiegsgesellschaft. Über das Aufbegehren in der regresssiven Moderne*, Berlin: Suhrkamp, 2016 (English translation forthcoming).
5 Ralf Dahrendorf, 'Anmerkungen zur Globalisierung', in Ulrich Beck (ed.), *Perspektiven der Weltgesellschaft*, Frankfurt am Main: Suhrkamp, 1998, pp. 41–54, here 52f.
6 Richard Rorty, *Achieving Our Country: Leftist Thought in Twentieth-Century America*, Cambridge, MA: Harvard University Press, 1998, especially Chapter 4, 'A Cultural Left', pp. 73–111, here 83–7.
7 Wilhelm Heitmeyer, 'Autoritärer Kapitalismus, Demokratisierung und Rechtspopulismus. Eine Analyse von Entwicklungstendenzen', in Dietmar Loch and Wilhelm Heitmeyer (eds), *Schattenseiten der Globalisierung. Rechtsradikalismus, Rechtspopulismus und separatistischer Regionalismus in westlichen Demokratien*, Frankfurt am Main: Suhrkamp 1998, pp. 497–534, here 500.
8 Dani Rodrik, *Has Globalization Gone Too Far?*, Washington, DC: Institute for International Economics, 1997, p. 86. In this context we could also mention Benjamin R. Barber, *Jihad vs. McWorld*, New York: Crown, 1995; Noam Chomsky, *Profit Over People*, New York: Seven Stories Press, 1999; Viviane

Forrester, *The Economic Horror*, Cambridge: Polity Press, 1999; Robert B. Reich, *The Work of Nations*, New York: Vintage Books, 1992; Harald Schumann and Hans-Peter Martin, *The Global Trap*, London: Pluto Press, 1997; Joseph E. Stiglitz, *Globalization and its Discontents*, London: Allen Lane, 2002.

9 Karl Polanyi, *The Great Transformation*, New York: Farrar and Rinehart, 1944.

10 On this point see – with explicit reference to Polanyi – Philip G. Cerny, 'Globalisierung und die neue Logik kollektiven Handelns', in Ulrich Beck (ed.), *Politik der Globalisierung*, Frankfurt am Main: Suhrkamp, 1998, pp. 263–96.

11 Accompanied at the time by further influential journalistic and theoretical diagnoses; we need think only of Naomi Klein, *No Logo: Taking Aim at the Brand Bullies*, Toronto: Knopf Canada, 1999, or Michael Hardt and Antonio Negri, *Empire*, Cambridge, MA and London: Harvard University Press, 2001.

12 See, among others, Ulrich Beck, *The Cosmopolitan Vision*, translated by Ciaran Cronin, Cambridge: Polity, 2006.

13 Böckenförde writes, albeit in a different context, 'The libertarian, secularised state lives on assumptions that it is unable to guarantee itself', in *Staat, Gesellschaft, Freiheit. Studien zur Staatstheorie und zum Verfassungsrecht*, Frankfurt am Main: Suhrkamp, 1977 [1967], pp. 42–64, here 60.

1

Democracy fatigue

Arjun Appadurai

The central question of our times is whether we are witnessing the worldwide rejection of liberal democracy and its replacement by some sort of populist authoritarianism. Strong signs of this trend are to be found in Trump's America, Putin's Russia, Modi's India and Erdoğan's Turkey. In addition, we have numerous examples of already existing authoritarian governments (Orbán in Hungary, Duda in Poland) and major aspirants to authoritarian right-wing rule in France, Austria and other European Union countries. The total population of these countries is almost a third of the total population of the world. There has been growing alarm about this global shift to the right but we have relatively few good explanations for it. In this essay, I offer an explanation and a European approach to building an alternative.

Leaders and followers

We need to rethink the relationship between leaders and followers in the new populisms that surround us. Our traditional habits of analysis lead us to imagine that major social trends in the political sphere have to do with such things as charisma, propaganda, ideology and other factors, all of which presume a strong connection between leaders and followers. Today, leaders and followers do of course connect but this connection is based on an accidental and partial overlap between the ambitions, visions and strategies of leaders and the fears, wounds and angers of their followers. The leaders who have risen in the new populist movements are typically xenophobic, patriarchal and authoritarian in their styles. Their followers may share some of these tendencies but they are also fearful, angry, and resentful of what their societies have done for and to them. These profiles do of course meet, especially in elections (however rigged or managed they may be). But this meeting place is not easy to understand. Why did some Muslims in India and the United States vote for Modi and Trump? Why do some women in the United States adore Trump? Why do groups from the former German Democratic Republic now vote for right-wing politicians? Addressing these puzzles requires us to think about leaders and followers in the new populisms somewhat independently of one another.

The message from above

The new populist leaders recognize that they aspire to national leadership in an era in which national sovereignty is in crisis. The most striking symptom of this crisis of sovereignty is that no modern nation-state controls what could be called its national economy. This is equally a problem for the richest and poorest of nations. The US economy is substantially in Chinese hands, the Chinese depend crucially on raw materials from Africa and Latin America as well as other parts of Asia, everyone depends to some extent on Middle Eastern oil, and virtually all modern nation-states depend on sophisticated armaments from a small number of wealthy countries. Economic sovereignty, as a basis for national sovereignty, was always a dubious principle. Today, it is increasingly irrelevant.

In the absence of any national economy that modern states can claim to protect and develop, it is no surprise that there has been a worldwide tendency in effective states and in many aspiring populist movements to perform national sovereignty by turning towards cultural majoritarianism, ethno-nationalism and the stifling of internal intellectual and cultural dissent. In other words, the loss of economic sovereignty everywhere produces a shift towards emphasizing cultural sovereignty. This turn towards culture as the site of national sovereignty appears in many forms.

Take Russia in the hands of Vladimir Putin. In December 2014, Putin signed a decree setting up a state cultural policy for Russia centred on the maxim 'Russia is not Europe'. Reflecting an explicit hostility to the cultural West and to European multiculturalism, which Putin has characterized as 'neutered and barren'[1] – both loaded sexual expressions – it enlists Russian masculinity as a political force. This rhetoric is an explicit call to return to traditional Russian values and is anchored on a deep history of Slavophile sentiment and Russophile cultural politics. The immediate context for this document was the battle over the future of Ukraine, and it underlay the cancellation of concerts by Russian anti-Kremlin rock musician Andrey Makarevich, while reflecting the longer-term harassment of the musical group Pussy Riot. The policy calls for a 'unified cultural space' throughout Russia and makes it clear that Russian cultural uniqueness and uniformity are crucial tools to be used against cultural minorities at home and political enemies abroad.

Turkey under Recep Tayyip Erdoğan has also turned culture into a theatre of sovereignty. The main vehicle of his strategy is to advocate a return to Ottoman traditions, language forms and imperial grandeur (an ideology that his critics have dubbed 'neo-Ottomanism'). This vision of Turkey also encodes its global ambitions, its resistance to Russian interventions in the Middle East, and acts as a counterweight to the country's aspiration to join the European Union. This neo-Ottoman posture is a key part of Erdoğan's endeavour to marginalize and replace the secular nationalism of Kemal Atatürk, the icon of modern Turkey, with a more religious and imperial style of rule. The country has also witnessed considerable censorship of art and cultural institutions alongside direct repression of popular political dissent, as in Gezi Park in 2013.

In many ways, Narendra Modi, the right-wing ideologue who now enjoys the prime ministership of India, offers the best example of how the new authoritarian leaders produce

and maintain a populist strategy. Modi has a long career as
a party worker and activist for the Hindu Right in India.
He served as chief minister of Gujarat from 2001 to 2014,
and was implicated in the state-wide genocide of Muslims
in Gujarat in 2002, after some Muslims attacked a train
carrying Hindu pilgrims through the state. Many progressive Indians still believe that Modi actively orchestrated this
genocide, but he has managed to overcome many judicial
and civil condemnations and won the campaign to become
prime minister of India in 2014. He is an open advocate of
Hindutva (Hindu nationalism) as the governing ideology of
India and, like many of the current crop of authoritarian
populists across the world, combines extreme cultural nationalism with markedly neoliberal policies and projects. Under
his now almost three-year-old leadership, there has been an
unprecedented number of assaults on sexual, religious, cultural and artistic freedoms in India, anchored in a systematic
dismantling of the secular and socialist heritage of Jawaharlal
Nehru and the non-violent vision of Mahatma Gandhi. Under
Modi, war with Pakistan is always a heartbeat away, India's
Muslims are living in growing fear, and Dalits (the lowest
castes, previously 'Untouchable') are brazenly attacked and
humiliated every day. Modi has brought together the lexicon
of ethnic purity with the discourse of cleanliness and sanita-
tion. Indian cultural images abroad, highlighting its combination of digital modernity and Hindu authenticity, and
Hindu domination at home are the cornerstones of Indian
sovereignty.

And so it is with our latest nightmare, the victory of
Donald Trump in the US elections of 8 November 2016. This
event is still very recent, so even hindsight is in poor supply.
But Trump has already begun to act on his election plans
with his cabinet appointments and policy utterances since his
election. We cannot expect his victory to moderate his style.
Trump's message, which combines misogyny, racism, xenophobia and megalomania on a scale unprecedented in recent
history, is centred on two extreme messages, one implicit
and one explicit. The explicit message is his aim to 'Make
America Great Again', by beefing up foreign military options
for the United States, renegotiating various trade deals that
he believes have diminished American wealth and prestige,

unshackling US businesses from various tax and environmental constraints, and, above all, by making good on his promises to 'register' all Muslims in the US, deport all illegals, tighten up American borders and massively increase immigration controls. The implicit message is racist and racial, and speaks to those white Americans who feel they have lost their imagined dominance in American politics and economy to blacks, Latinos and migrants of every type. Trump's biggest rhetorical success is to put the Greeks of 'whiteness' into the Trojan horse of every one of his messages about 'American' greatness, so that 'making America great again' becomes the public way of promising that whites in America will be great again. For the first time, a message about America's power in the world has become a dog-whistle for making whites the ruling class of and in the US again. The message about the salvation of the American economy has been transformed into a message about saving the white race.

This, then, is what the leaders of the new authoritarian populisms have in common: the recognition that none of them can truly control their national economies, which are hostages to foreign investors, global agreements, transnational finance, mobile labour and capital in general. All of them promise national cultural purification as a route to global political power. All of them are friendly to neoliberal capitalism, with their own versions of how to make it work for India, Turkey, the United States or Russia. All of them seek to translate soft power into hard power. And none of them has any reservations about repressing minorities and dissidents, stifling free speech or using the law to throttle their opponents.

This worldwide package is also visible in Europe, in Theresa May's UK, Victor Orbán's Hungary, Andrzej Duda's Poland, and in a host of increasingly vocal and 'mainstream' right-wing parties in virtually every other country. In Europe, the flashpoints for this trend are the fear of the latest wave of migrants, the anger about the various terrorist attacks in some of its major cities, and, of course, the shock of the Brexit vote. Thus populist authoritarian leaders and demagogues are to be found everywhere across the old continent, and they too operate with the same mix of neoliberalism, cultural chauvinism, anti-immigrant anger and majoritarian rage as the major models discussed in this essay.

This is one way to look at the leaders of the new authoritarian populisms and their appeals. What about the followers?

Vox populi

I suggested earlier that an explanation of the worldwide success of populist authoritarians should not assume that the followers simply endorse or replicate the beliefs of the leaders they seem to adore. There is, of course, a degree of overlap or compatibility between what these leaders decry or promise and what their followers believe or fear. But the overlap is partial, and the popular followings that have allowed Modi, Putin, Erdoğan and Trump, as well as May, Orbán and Duda in Europe, to achieve and retain power have their own worlds of belief, affect and motivation. To grasp something of what these worlds are like, I return to the famous ideas put forward by the political economist and philosopher Albert O. Hirschman in his brilliant book *Exit, Voice, and Loyalty*.[2] Hirschman provides a powerful understanding of how human beings respond to a decline in products, organizations and states by either remaining loyal to them, leaving them or staying with them to protest the decline by 'voicing' opposition, resistance or complaints in the hope of repair or reform. The great originality of Hirschman's analysis was its linking of consumer behaviour to organizational and political behaviour, and his approach was a vital move in comprehending how long and in what circumstances ordinary people could tolerate disappointment with goods and services before they switched brands, membership of organizations, or countries. Published in 1970, Hirschman's book offered a deep insight into modern capitalist democracies before globalization began to undo the logic of national economies, local communities and place-based identities. It was also written before the rise of the internet and social media and thus could not have anticipated the nature of disappointment and protest in the world of the twenty-first century.

Still, Hirschman's ideas remind us that Brexit is above all about exit and that exit is always in some kind of relationship to loyalty and to voice. How can Hirschman's use of these terms help us today? I suggest that from the perspective of those mass followings that support Trump, Modi, Erdoğan and the other established or rising figures of authoritarian populism, the exit that far too many of them are today supporting is a form of voice, not an alternative to it. More concretely, Hirschman was right that elections were the major way in which citizens enacted voice and showed how disappointed or happy they were with their leaders. But elections today – and the recent US elections are an excellent example – have become a way to 'exit' from democracy itself, rather than a means to repair and debate politics democratically. The approximately sixty-two million Americans who voted for Trump voted for him and against democracy. In this sense their vote was a vote for 'exit'. And so it was with the election of Modi, the election of Erdoğan and the pseudo-elections in favour of Putin.

In each of these cases, and in many of the populist pockets of Europe, there is a fatigue with democracy itself, a fatigue which forms the basis for the electoral success of leaders who promise to abrogate all the liberal, deliberative and inclusive components of their national versions of democracy. It might be objected that all populist leaders have thrived on this sort of frustration with democracy and have built their careers on it, going back to Stalin, Hitler, Peron and the many other leaders from the first half of the twentieth century who exploited the failures of the democracies of their times and places. So what is new about today's democracy fatigue?

There are three ways in which today's widespread feeling of being fed up with democracy itself has a distinctive logic and context. The first is that the extension of the internet and social media to growing sectors of the population and the availability of web-based mobilization, propaganda, identity-building and peer-seeking have created the dangerous illusion that we can all find peers, allies, friends, collaborators, converts and colleagues, whoever we are and whatever we want. The second is the fact that every single nation-state has lost ground in its efforts to maintain any semblance of economic sovereignty. The third factor is that the worldwide spread of the ideology of human rights has given some minimal purchase to strangers, foreigners and migrants in virtually every country in the world, even if they face a harsh welcome and

severe conditions wherever they go. Together, these three
factors have deepened the global intolerance for due process,
deliberative rationality and political patience that democratic
systems always require. When we add to these factors the
worldwide deepening of economic inequality, the global
erosion of social welfare, and the planetary penetration of
financial industries that thrive on circulating the idea that we
are all at risk of financial disaster, impatience with the slow
temporalities of democracy is compounded by a constant
climate of economic panic. The same populist leaders who
promise prosperity for all often deliberately create this sort
of panic. Narendra Modi's recent decision to root out 'black
money' (untaxed cash wealth) from the Indian economy by
taking 500 and 1,000 rupee currency notes out of circulation is an exemplary case of induced economic distress and
financial panic. In today's India these currency notes are a
vital part of everyday life for poor and middle-class workers,
consumers and petty commercial operators, since they are
worth about 7 and 14 euros respectively.

The new chapter being written in the worldwide story of
authoritarian populism is thus founded on a partial overlap
between the ambitions and promises of its leaders and the
mentality of its followers. The leaders hate democracy because
it is an obstacle to their monomaniacal pursuit of power. The
followers are victims of democracy fatigue who see electoral
politics as the best way to exit democracy itself. This hatred
and this exhaustion find their natural common ground in
the space of cultural sovereignty, enacted in scripts of racial
victory for resentful majorities, national ethnic purity and
global resurgence through the promises of soft power. This
common cultural ground inevitably hides the deep contradictions between the neoliberal economic policies and well-
documented crony capitalism of most of these authoritarian
leaders and the genuine economic suffering and anxiety of
the bulk of their mass followings. It is also the terrain of a
new politics of exclusion, whose targets are either migrants or
internal ethnic minorities or both. As long as jobs, pensions
and incomes continue to shrink, minorities and migrants will
continue to be obvious scapegoats until a persuasive political
message emerges from left liberal voices about restructuring
income, social welfare and public resources. To be realistic,

this is not a short-term project, but it has to be a medium-term priority of the highest order. Here, since Europe is on the cutting edge, I conclude by returning to the old continent.

Where is Europe headed?

The consequences of the Brexit vote are still playing out. But its outcome indicates a mood in Europe that is not unrelated to the global trend to the right and to a growing ambivalence about the EU in many of its member states. Leaving aside the details of UK politics, some general observations come to mind.

The first is that Brexit is only the most recent version of a long and recurrent debate about what Europe is and what it means. This debate is as old as the idea of Europe itself. The question of Europe's boundaries, identity and mission has never been resolved. Is Europe a project of Western Christendom? Is it the child of Roman law and empire? Or of Greek rationality and democratic values? Or of Renaissance humanism and secularism? Or of Enlightenment universalism and cosmopolitanism? These alternative images have struggled with one another for centuries and remain the subjects of deep division. They are images espoused by different classes, regions, states and intellectuals at different times, and none of them has ever been completely hegemonic. Neither has any of them moved out of the picture entirely. They have also coexisted with bloody internal wars, massive religious schisms, and brutal efforts to eliminate minorities, strangers, heretics and political dissidents. This combination of factors continues to be relevant today.

It is not difficult to see that the fear of new immigrants (as well as of existing migrant populations) is a major part of the recent growth of arguments against the EU in its core countries, such as France, Holland and Germany, as well as in Poland, Hungary and Slovenia, which resent the efforts of the EU leadership in Brussels to dictate quotas, criteria and legal categories in relation to refugees and other migrants to countries facing the immediate impact of new arrivals. It is also evident that this resentment is compounded by the sense that membership in the Union represents a net loss for economic well-being in many of its member countries, and that an exit would thus be in their best interests. But such exits are doomed efforts to regain the sort of economic sovereignty which is impossible to restore in the current era of globalization. Indeed, the debate over migrants (often at the forefront of right-wing political movements and agendas in Europe) is a prime example of the translation of issues of economic sovereignty into issues of cultural sovereignty, a translation and displacement which I have argued lies at the heart of the growth of right-wing populisms worldwide.

In Europe, the variety of movements that endorse some sort of 'exit' from the EU are also those that are using electoral processes to exit from democracy, in the manner that I have argued is the case in the United States, India, Russia and Turkey. What the European cases of democracy fatigue bring most sharply to our attention is the wish of many political groups and movements to harvest the benefits of globalization without the burdens of democracy. In the case of Britain, for example, membership in the European Union became associated with liberal ideology at home. Thus, Theresa May's recent visit to India for discussions with Narendra Modi offers a revealing glimpse of the future of global neoliberalism in a world unburdened by democracy. The two leaders agreed on issues of cross-border terrorism (meaning Pakistan) and British financial investments in Indian infrastructure, but had tough words for one another on the question of Indian student visa quotas in the UK and the status of Indians who 'overstay' their visas in England. Hence a Tory leader who rose to power on the Brexit vote and an Indian right-wing populist authoritarian of world rank are already doing business over how to ensure the free flow of international capital while horse-trading over visas and migrants. This is a glimpse of how business will be done between the new authoritarian leaders of the world when they are no longer burdened by democracy at home and when they have been propelled into power by mass followings suffering from democracy fatigue. Trump and Putin already have cosy ties, and Modi's and Trump's followers among Indians in the United States are already closely allied.

European liberal democracy is on the verge of a dangerous crisis. Democracy fatigue has arrived in Europe, and is visible from Sweden to Italy and from France to Hungary. In Europe too, elections are becoming ways to say 'no' to liberal democracy. In this scenario, Germany is at a major and risky crossroads. It can use its remarkable wealth, economic stability and historical self-consciousness to hold up the ideals of the European Union, to offer a welcome to refugees from Africa and the Middle East, to pursue peaceful solutions to global political crises, and to use the power of the euro to expand the scope of equality both within its borders and in Europe more generally. Or it can also exit, close its borders, hoard its wealth and let the rest of Europe (and the world) solve its own problems. The latter may be the message from the German right, but it would be a foolish option. Global interdependence is here to stay and German wealth is as dependent on the global economy as anyone else's. The 'exit' solution would not be good for Germany. It has no choice but to push for a democratic Europe, and a democratic Europe is a vital resource in the worldwide struggle against authoritarian populism.

But for this scenario to work, Germany will have to convince its fellow EU members that it will not be the voice of austerity and imposed financial discipline, especially in Southern and Eastern Europe. In other words, a soft policy on migrants and cultural tolerance at home is not consistent with a harsh approach to internal European debt and a dramatic reduction in fiscal sovereignty for countries like Greece, Spain and Italy. This is a tricky problem because German wealth also depends on a strong euro, and without German wealth German liberalism is unlikely to survive. The challenge here is whether Germany can support the forces of liberal democracy in those European countries that threaten to move to the right, and whether this is possible without putting Germany (again) in the role of a European hegemon. There is no easy answer to this dilemma but it is not one to avoid. German liberal democracy cannot survive in an ocean of European authoritarian populism. So, in the end, there is only one path ahead and that is for European liberal publics (workers, intellectuals, activists, policy makers) to make common cause across European internal borders to argue for economic and political liberalism. We need a liberal multitude. That is the only answer to the regressive multitude which is currently on the rise in Europe and beyond.

Arjun Appadurai

Notes

1 Vladimir Putin, Presidential Address to the Federal Assembly, 12 December 2014. An English translation of the speech is available at http://en.kremlin.ru/events/president/news/19825 (retrieved November 2016).
2 Albert O. Hirschman, *Exit, Voice, and Loyalty: Responses to Decline in Firms, Organizations, and States*, Cambridge, MA: Harvard University Press, 1970.

2

Symptoms in search of an object and a name

Zygmunt Bauman

> I hear the sound of a trumpet, and I asked my servant what it meant. He knew nothing and had heard nothing. At the gate he stopped me and asked: 'Where is the master going?' 'I don't know', I said, 'just out of here, just out of here. Out of here, nothing else, it's the only way I can reach my goal.' 'So you know your goal?' he asked. 'Yes', I replied. 'I've just told you. Out of here – that is my goal.'
>
> Kafka, 'The Departure'[1]

When a growing number of people hear trumpets, become restless and go on the run, two questions can, need and indeed tend to be asked: Where are these people running *from*? And where are they running *to*? Servants would suppose their masters to know, and, as Kafka suggested, would ask and insist on being told their destination. Masters, however, at least the most circumspect and responsible among them, and above all the most far-sighted (those eager to learn from the bitter experience of Paul Klee's/Walter Benjamin's Angel of History, known to be irresistibly propelled into the future to which his back is turned, as the pile of debris rises before him, his eyes fixed tightly on the repellent, all-too-palpable inanities and horrors of the past and present, capable at best of speculating and fantasizing on his destination), are likely to dodge giving a straight answer, assuming that the 'where from' is as far as they dare go in attempting to explain. They are aware that they have more than enough reasons for running, but that they run with their backs turned to the Great Unknown, with too few hints to anticipate their destination. But such an answer would leave the servants nonplussed. If anything, it would raise their anxiety and anger levels to a pitch of panic and fury.

Today we feel that all the expedients and stratagems we took until recently to be effective – if not foolproof when it came to resisting and tackling the dangers of crises – have passed or are about to pass their use-by date. But we have little if any inkling of what to replace them with. The hope of taking history under human management, and the resulting determination to do so, have all but vanished, as the successive leaps and bounds of human history have vied with, and come to outdo, natural catastrophes in their unexpectedness and uncontrollability.

If we still believe in 'progress' (by no means a foregone conclusion), we tend to view it now as a mixture of blessing and curse, the curses growing steadily in volume as the blessings become ever fewer and farther between. While our recent ancestors still believed in the future as the safest and most promising location for investing their hopes, we tend to project into it primarily our manifold fears, anxieties and apprehensions: of the growing scarcity of jobs, of falling incomes reducing our and our children's life chances, of the yet greater frailty of our social positions and the temporality of our life achievements, of the increasingly widening gap between the tools, resources and skills at our disposal and the momentousness of the challenges facing us. Above all, we feel our control over our own lives slipping from our hands, reducing us to the status of pawns moved to and fro in a chess game played by unknown players indifferent to our needs, if not downright hostile and cruel, and all too ready to sacrifice us in pursuit of their own objectives. Not so long ago associated with more comfort and less inconvenience, what the thought of the future tends nowadays to bring to mind most often is the gruesome menace of being identified or classified as inept and unfit for the task, denied value and dignity, and for that reason marginalized, excluded and outcast.

Let me focus on one of the symptoms of our current condition – the recently staged, and in all likelihood still far from
complete drama of the 'immigration panic' – treating it as
a window through which certain frightening aspects of our
situation that might otherwise remain hidden can be spied
out.

There is, for a start, *emigration/immigration* (from/to).
And there is *migration* (from, but where to?). They are ruled
by different sets of laws and logics, the difference having
been determined by the divergence of their roots. All the
same, there is a similarity between their effects, dictated by
the nature of the psychosocial conditions in the destination
countries. Both the differences and the similarities are mag-
nified by the ongoing, and in all probability unstoppable,
globalization of economy and information. The former turns
all genuinely or putatively sovereign territories into 'com-
municating vessels', between which their liquid contents are
known to keep flowing until an equal level is reached in all.
The latter stretches the stimuli diffusion, copycat behaviour,
and the areas and yardsticks of 'relative deprivation' to a fully
and truly planet-wide dimension.

The phenomenon of immigration, as the uniquely visionary Umberto Eco pointed out well before the present-day
migration of peoples took off, 'may be controlled politically,
restricted, encouraged, planned, or accepted. This is not the
case with migration'.² Eco then asks the crucial question:
'Is it possible to distinguish immigration from migration
when the entire planet is becoming the territory of intersect-
ing movements of people?' And as he suggests in his reply:
'What Europe is still trying to tackle as immigration is in fact
migration. The Third World is knocking at our doors, and
it will come in, even if we are not in agreement. ... Europe
will become a multiracial continent – or "coloured" one ...
That's how it will be, whether you like it or not.' And, let
me add, whether *all* of 'them' like it and/or *all* of 'us' resent
it.

At what point does emigration/immigration turn into
migration? At what point does the politically manageable
trickle of immigrants knocking-at-our-doors turn into the
massive quasi-self-sustained and self-propelling influx of
migrants overflowing or by-passing all doors, complete with

their hastily patched together political reinforcements? At what point do the quantitative additions turn into qualitative changes? The answers to such questions are bound to remain essentially contested well beyond the moment that might retrospectively be recognized as having been the watershed.

What sets the two phenomena apart is the issue of 'assimilation': its endemic presence in the concept of immigration and its conspicuous absence in the concept of migration – a void filled initially by the notions of 'melting pot' or 'hybridization', and now, increasingly, by that of 'multiculturalism', i.e., of a cultural differentiation and diversity set to stay for the foreseeable future, rather than being a stage on the road to cultural homogeneity and so, essentially, no more than a temporary irritant. To avoid any confusion between the extant state of affairs and the policies intended to tackle it – a kind of befuddlement for which the concept of 'multiculturalism' is infamous – it is advisable to replace the latter term with the concept of 'diasporization'. This is suggestive of two crucial traits of the state of affairs currently emerging as a result of migration – a state much more subject to grassroots processes and influences than it is dependent on top-down regulation, and one that grounds the interaction between diasporas more on the division of labour than on a gelling of cultures.

Eco published his essay in 1997. In 1990, the city of New York, which he used as an example, counted 43 per cent 'whites', 29 per cent 'blacks', 21 per cent 'Hispanics' and 7 per cent 'Asians' among its population. Twenty years later, in 2010, 'whites' made up only 33 per cent and were edging ever nearer to becoming a minority.[3] A very similar number of distinct ethnic, religious or linguistic categories, with a similar distribution of percentages, can be recorded in all the world's major cities, whose number is also on the rise. And let us recall that for the first time in history most of humanity lives in cities, while most of that urbanized part of humanity resides in large cities, where life patterns for the rest of the planet tend to be set and modified on a daily basis.

Whether we like it or not, we the urban dwellers find ourselves in a situation that requires us to develop the skills of living with difference daily, and in all probability permanently.

After a couple of centuries dreaming of cultural assimilation (unilateral) or convergence (bilateral), and the ensuing practices, we are beginning to face up – if in many cases reluctantly, and often with unmitigated resistance – to the prospect of the mixture of interaction and friction between the multiplicity of irreducibly diverse identities involved in neighbouring and/or intermixed cultural diasporas. Cultural heterogeneity is fast becoming an irremovable, indeed endemic, trait of the urban mode of human cohabitation, but realization of such a prospect does not come easy and the first response is one of denial – or a resolute, emphatic and pugnacious rejection.

Intolerance, Eco suggests,

> comes before any doctrine. In this sense intolerance has biological roots, it manifests itself among animals as territoriality, it is based on emotional reactions that are often superficial – we cannot bear those who are different from us, because their skin is of different colour; because they speak a language we do not understand; because they eat frogs, dogs, monkeys, pigs or garlic; because they tattoo themselves ...[4]

Putting still stronger emphasis on the main reason for this stark opposition to common beliefs, Eco reiterates: 'doctrines of difference do not produce uncontrolled intolerance: on the contrary, they exploit a pre-existing and diffuse reservoir of intolerance'.[5] Such a statement chimes well with the insistence of Fredrik Barth, the formidable Norwegian anthropologist, that boundaries are not drawn because of noted differences, but the other way round – differences are noted or invented because boundaries have already been drawn. According to both thinkers, doctrines are composed to 'rationally' explain and justify, retrospectively, the already present and in most cases firmly settled ill-disposed, disapproving, antagonistic, resentful and bellicose emotions.

Eco goes so far as to say that the 'most dangerous form' of intolerance is that which arises in the absence of any doctrine.[6] One can, after all, engage in polemics with an articulated doctrine to disprove its explicit assertions and expose its latent presumptions one by one. Elemental drives, however, are immune to, and insulated against, such arguments.

Fundamentalist, integralist, racist and ethnically chauvinist demagogues may be, and need to be, charged with feeding and capitalizing on the pre-existing 'elemental intolerance' for political gain, thereby widening its reverberations and exacerbating its morbidity – but they cannot be charged with *causing* the phenomenon of intolerance.

Where to look, therefore, for the origin and mainspring of that phenomenon? In the last account, I suggest, to the fear of the *unknown* – of which the 'strangers' or 'aliens' (by definition insufficiently known, still less understood, and all but unpredictable in their conduct and responses to one's own gambits) are the most prominent emblems: the most tangible because nearby and conspicuous. On the world map on which we inscribe our destinations and the roads leading to them, they stay uncharted (again by definition: had they been charted, they would have been moved to some category other than that of the stranger). Their status is uncannily reminiscent of that signalled on ancient maps by the warning *hic sunt leones*, inscribed on the outskirts of the inhabitable and inhabited οἴκουμένη – with the proviso, though, that these mysterious, sinister and intimidating beasts, lions in migrant disguise, have by now left their distant lairs and squatted, surreptitiously, next door. If in the era when these maps were sketched one could prudently avoid venturing near their dens and by such a simple stratagem steer clear of trouble, such an option is no longer available. 'The beasts' are now at our doors, and one can't avoid encountering them whenever one steps out onto the street.

To sum up: in the world in which we live, one can attempt to control immigration (if with only minor success), but migration is bound to follow its own logic whatever we do. The process will continue for a long time to come – alongside another, wider, and arguably the most consequential, transformation the human condition is currently undergoing. This other problem – as Ulrich Beck, the greatest social analyst of the manifest and latent trends in the human condition at the turn from the twentieth to the twenty-first century and of their foreseeable prospects, suggested – is the jarring contradiction between our already-close-to-cosmopolitan *plight* and the virtual absence of a cosmopolitan *awareness*, mindset or attitude. This problem lies at the root of our most nagging current quandaries and most unsettling concerns and worries. By our 'cosmopolitan plight' Beck meant the advanced, already worldwide, material and spiritual interdependence of humanity, elsewhere called globalization. Between that plight and our capacity to adjust our actions to its unprecedented demands, a wide and thus far unbridgeable gap extends. We are still left with instruments designed in the past to service the conditions of autonomy, independence and sovereignty, to tackle (in itself an impossible task!) the headaches arising from the already-reached condition of interdependence, erosion and watering down of territorial autonomy and sovereignty.

There are conceivably many legitimate, if condensed and simplified, ways in which the story of humankind might be recapitulated, and one among them is the story of the sometimes piecemeal, sometimes abrupt extension of 'we' – starting from the hordes of hunter-gatherers (which, according to palaeontologists, couldn't have included more than about 150 members), through the 'imagined totalities' of tribes and empires, and up to contemporary nation-states or 'superstates' in their federations or coalitions. None of the extant political formations, however, measures up to a genuinely 'cosmopolitan' standard; all of them pair a 'we' against a 'them'. Each member of that opposition combines a uniting or integrating function with a dividing and separating one – indeed, each can perform one of the two assigned functions by and through acquitting itself from the other.

This division of humans into 'us' and 'them' – their juxtaposition and antagonism – has been an inseparable feature of the human mode of being-in-the-world throughout the history of the species. 'Us' and 'them' are related as heads *and* tails – two faces of the same coin; and a coin with only one face is an oxymoron, a contradiction in terms. The two members of the opposition are reciprocally 'negatively defined': 'them' as 'not-us', and 'we' as 'not-them'.

Such a mechanism worked well enough during earlier stages of the progressive expansion of politically integrated bodies – but it does not square well with its latest phase, imposed on the political agenda by the emergent 'cosmopolitan condition'. Indeed, it is singularly unfit for performing 'the last leap' in the history of human integration: raising the 'we' concept and the practices of human cohabitation, cooperation and solidarity to the level of humanity as a whole. That last leap stands out starkly from the long history of its smaller-scale antecedents as not just *quantitatively* but *qualitatively* distinct, unprecedented and untested in practice. It calls for nothing less than a necessarily traumatic separation of the issue of 'belonging' (that is, of self-identification) from that of territoriality or political sovereignty: a postulate voiced loudly a hundred or so years ago by the likes of Otto Bauer, Karl Reiner and Vladimir Menem in response to the multinational realities of the Austro-Hungarian and Russian empires, though never coming anywhere close to entering into political usage or convention.

Application of that postulate doesn't seem on the cards in the foreseeable future. On the contrary: most of the current symptoms[7] point to an increasingly ardent search for 'them' – preferably the old-fashioned, unmistakable and incurably hostile alien, fit for the job of identity-reinforcement, boundary-drawing and wall-building. The impulsive 'natural' and routine reaction of a growing number of powers-that-be to the progressive erosion of their territorial sovereignty tends to involve a loosening of their supra-state commitments and a retreat from their previous consent to pooling resources and coordinating policies – thus moving them yet further away from complementing and matching their objectively cosmopolitan plight with programmes and undertakings at a similar level. Such a state of affairs only adds to the global disarray underpinning the gradual yet relentless disabling of the extant institutions of political power. The prime winners are extraterritorial financiers, investment funds and commodity traders of all shades of legality, while the main losers are economic and social equality, principles of inner- and inter-state justice, together with a large part, possibly a growing majority, of the world's population.

Instead of an earnest, consistent, coordinated and long-term undertaking to uproot the resulting existential fears, governments across the globe have jumped at the chance of filling the vacuum of legitimacy left behind by shrinking social provisions and the abandonment of post-war efforts to institute a 'family of nations' with a powerful push towards the 'securitization' of social problems and, in consequence, of political thought and action. Popular fears, stoked, aided and abetted by an unwritten but intimate alliance of political elites, mass information and entertainment media, and spurred yet further by the rising tide of demagoguery, are to all intents and purposes welcomed as a most precious ore fit for the continuous smelting of fresh supplies of political capital – a capital coveted by off-the-leash commercial powers and their political lobbies and executors who have been famished of its more orthodox varieties.

From the top to the bottom of society – incorporating labour markets that set the tune played by their pipers for us, the *hoi polloi*, to sing along to – a climate of mutual (and a priori) mistrust, suspiciousness and cut-throat competition is created. In such a climate the germs of communal spirit and mutual help suffocate, wilt and fade (if their buds have not already been forcibly nipped out). With the stakes in concerted, solidary actions in the common interest losing their value day in, day out, and their potential effects dimming, the interest in joining forces and attending to shared interests in common is robbed of most of its attraction and so the stimuli to engage in a dialogue aimed at reciprocal recognition, respect and bona fide understanding are dying out.

'If states ever become large neighbourhoods, it is likely that neighbourhoods will become little states. Their members will organize to defend the local politics and culture against strangers. Historically, neighbourhoods have turned into closed or parochial communities … whenever the state was open' – so Michael Walzer concluded over thirty years ago, from the by then accumulated experience of the past, presaging its repetition in the imminent future.[8] That future, having turned into the present, has only confirmed his expectations and diagnosis.

Whether big or little, being a state has the same simple meaning: territorial sovereignty, i.e., the capacity to act inside one's own borders as the inhabitants of those borders wish, rather than at someone else's behest. After an era of neighbourhoods melting, or viewed as destined to melt, into larger units called nation-states (with the prospect of the unification and homogenization of human culture/law/politics/ life lurking, if not in an immediate, then in an irreversibly impending, future), after the protracted war declared by the big on the small, by the state on the local and 'parochial', we enter the epoch of 'subsidiarization', with states eager to offload their obligations, responsibilities and (courtesy of globalization and the emergent cosmopolitan situation) the cumbersome duty of recasting chaos into order, while yesterday's localities and parishes line up to grasp those responsibilities and to fight for still more. *The most conspicuous, conflict-pregnant and potentially explosive marker of the current moment is the intention to retreat from Kant's vision of a forthcoming* Bürgerliche Vereinigung der Menschheit, *coinciding with the realities of the advanced and escalating globalization of finance, industry, trade, information and all forms and shapes of law-breaking. Its close associate is the confrontation of a* Klein abermein *('small but mine') mindset and sentiment with the reality of an increasingly cosmopolitan existential condition.*

Indeed, as a result of globalization and the ensuing division of power and politics, states are presently turning into not much more than somewhat larger neighbourhoods, squeezed inside vaguely delineated, porous and ineffectually fortified borders; while the neighbourhoods of old – once assumed to be headed for the dustbin of history along with all the other *pouvoirs intermédiaires* – struggle to take on the role of 'little states', making the most of what is left of quasi-local politics and of the state's once jealously guarded and inalienable monopolist prerogative of setting 'us' apart from 'them' (and of course vice versa). 'Forward', for these little states, boils down to 'back to tribes'.

Within a territory populated by tribes, conflicting sides shun and doggedly desist from persuading, proselytizing or converting each other; the inferiority of a member – any member – of an alien tribe is and must remain a predestined liability, eternal and incurable, or at least be seen and treated as such. The inferiority of the other tribe is its ineffaceable and irreparable condition and its indelible stigma – bound to resist any attempt at rehabilitation. Once the division between 'us' and 'them' has been instituted according to such rules, the purpose of any encounter between the antagonists is no longer one of mitigation, but one of finding or creating further proofs that any such mitigation is contrary to reason and out of the question. In their endeavour to let sleeping dogs lie and avert misfortune, the members of different tribes locked in a superiority/inferiority loop talk not to but past each other.

In the case of the residents of (or exiles to) the grey frontier zones, the condition of 'being unknown and therefore menacing' is the effect of their inherent or imputed resistance to, or evasion of, the cognitive categories that serve as building blocks of 'order' and 'normality'. Their cardinal sin or unforgivable crime consists in being the cause of a mental and pragmatic incapacitation, itself a consequence of the behavioural confusion they cannot help but generate (here we might recall Ludwig Wittgenstein's definition of understanding as knowing how to go on). In addition, that sin encounters formidable obstacles to its redemption, given the stout refusal of 'us' to engage in a dialogue with 'them' aimed at defying and overcoming the initial impossibility of understanding. The assignment to a grey zone is a self-propelling process set in motion and intensified by the breakdown, or rather the a priori refusal, of communication. Raising the difficulty of understanding to the rank of a moral injunction and a duty predetermined by God or History is, after all, the prime cause of, and a paramount stimulus to, the drawing up and fortifying of borders separating 'us' from 'them', mostly though not exclusively along religious or ethnic lines, and the fundamental function they are ascribed to perform. As an interface between the two, the grey zone of ambiguity and ambivalence inevitably constitutes the major, perhaps even the main (and all too often the sole), territory on which the implacable hostilities between 'us' and 'them' are played out and the battles fought.

*

Pope Francis – perhaps the only public figure of worldwide authority to have had the courage and determination to dig down into the deepest sources of the present-day evil, confusion and impotence and put them on display – declared on the occasion of the conferral of the Charlemagne Prize for 2016 that:

> if there is one word that we should never tire of repeating, it is this: dialogue. We are called to promote a culture of dialogue by every possible means and thus to rebuild the fabric

of society. The culture of dialogue entails a true apprentice-
ship and a discipline that enables us to view others as valid
dialogue partners, to respect the foreigner, the immigrant and
people from different cultures as worthy of being listened to.
Today we urgently need to engage all the members of society
in building 'a culture which privileges dialogue as a form of
encounter' and in creating 'a means for building consensus
and agreement while seeking the goal of a just, responsive
and inclusive society' (*Evangelii Gaudium*, 239). Peace will
be lasting in the measure that we arm our children with
the weapons of dialogue, that we teach them to fight the
good fight of encounter and negotiation. In this way, we will
bequeath to them a culture capable of devising strategies of
life, not death, and of inclusion, not exclusion.[9]

And, right away, Pope Francis adds a sentence containing
another message inseparably connected to, indeed a *conditio
sine qua non* for, the culture of dialogue: 'This culture ...
should be an integral part of the education imparted in our
schools, cutting across disciplinary lines and helping to give
young people the tools needed to settle conflicts differently
than we are accustomed to do.'

Positing a culture of dialogue as the task of education, and
us in the role of teachers, unambiguously implies that the
problems now haunting us are here to stay for a long time
to come – problems that we will try in vain to settle in 'the
ways we are accustomed to', but for which the culture of
dialogue stands a chance of finding altogether more humane
(and hopefully effective) solutions. The old but in no way
outdated Chinese folk wisdom instructs those of us concerned
about the next year to sow grain; those worrying about the
next ten years to plant trees; and those who care about the
next hundred years to educate people.

The problems currently confronting us admit of no magic
wands, short cuts or instant cures; they call for nothing less
than another *cultural* revolution. Hence they also demand
long-term thought and planning: arts alas by and large forgotten, and seldom put into operation, in our hurried lives
lived under the tyranny of the moment. We need to recall and
relearn those arts. To do that, we will need cool heads, nerves
of steel and much courage; above all, we will need a full and
truly long-term vision – and a lot of patience.

Notes

1 Franz Kafka, 'The Departure', in *The Collected Short Stories of Franz Kafka*, London: Penguin, 1988, p. 449.
2 Umberto Eco, 'Migration, Tolerance, and the Intolerable', in *Five Moral Pieces*, London: Secker & Warburg, 2001, p. 93.
3 'The Changing Racial and Ethnic Makeup of New York City Neighborhoods', at http://furmancenter.org/files/sotc/The_Changing_Racial_and_Ethnic_Makeup_of_New_York_City_Neighborhoods_11.pdf#page=3&zoom=auto,-193,797 (retrieved November 2016).
4 Eco, 'Migration, Tolerance, and the Intolerable', pp. 99–100.
5 Ibid., p. 100.
6 Ibid., p. 101.
7 I list more such symptoms in my book *Retrotopia*, Cambridge: Polity, 2017.
8 Michael Walzer, *Spheres of Justice: A Defence of Pluralism and Equality*, New York: Basic Books, 1983, p. 38.
9 'Conferral of the Charlemagne Prize: Address of His Holiness Pope Francis', 6 May 2016, at http://w2.vatican.va/content/francesco/en/speeches/2016/may/documents/papa-francesco_20160506_premio-carlo-magno.html (retrieved November 2016).

3

Progressive and regressive politics in late neoliberalism

Donatella della Porta

Donald Trump's victory in the 2016 US presidential election has been widely perceived as a sign of the triumph of regressive over progressive movements. Similarly, the Brexit referendum has been taken as an indicator of a wave of parochialism that threatens to wash away a once-dominant cosmopolitan sentiment. While the turn of the century witnessed powerful mobilizations from the left such as the global justice movement (think of the so-called 'Battle of Seattle' in 1999, the first World Social Forum held in 2001 under the motto 'Another World Is Possible', or the emergence of organizations like Attac), and the 2008 financial crisis brought to the fore such anti-austerity movements as Occupy Wall Street and the *indignados* in Spain, the last few years have been characterized by the re-emergence of the dark side of politics. That said, it would be a mistake to forget that initial signs of reactionary movements were already visible in Europe fifteen years ago, when Jörg Haider's FPÖ came second place in the 1999 Austrian parliamentary elections, prompting a right-wing coalition government under chancellor Wolfgang Schüssel of the ÖVP. A few years later, in 2002, Jean-Marie Le Pen made it to the second round of the French presidential elections, where he ultimately lost to Jacques Chirac. Bearing those events in mind, it seems safe to conclude that discontent with neoliberal globalization has been present on both the left and the right for quite some time.

Research indicates that the social base of (left-wing) protest has shifted from the industrial working class, as was characteristic of the classical labour movement, to the new middle classes, which constituted the core of the new social movements of the 1960s and 1970s. The global justice movement, however, drew attention back to mobilizations conducted by the losers in the process of rampant neoliberal development that has been the hallmark of recent decades. From a social point of view, it has mobilized coalitions of white- and blue-collar workers, unemployed people and students, as well as younger and older generations.[1] At the same time, however, a populist right – building upon some of the grievances and conflicts related to the various facets of globalization – grew stronger as well. Numerous scholars have identified the emergence of a new cleavage between globalization's winners and losers, with the latter often opposing its cultural dimension through xenophobic and anti-immigrant claims that converge in exclusive forms of nationalism.[2]

It should come as no surprise that moments of crisis also engender political and social polarization. In fact, social movements have frequently emerged simultaneously on both the left *and* the right.[3] However, it remains to be seen whether the Brexit or Trump campaigns can truly be conceived of as populist *movements*, rather than as other forms of populist politics.

In what follows, I will first identify some of the main social challenges introduced by capitalist transformations; secondly, I will discuss some differences in the reactions those challenges have provoked thus far in terms of progressive and regressive politics; and thirdly, I will suggest some political conditions that might be conducive for the development of either of the two.

Neoliberal globalization as the challenge

Neoliberalism and its crisis can be understood within a framework that the political economist Karl Polanyi described as a double movement in the development of capitalism: when society experiences a push for marketization this is followed by the emergence of counter-movements seeking social protection. In his seminal book *The Great Transformation* (1944),

Polanyi actually addresses the initial nineteenth-century wave of liberalism,[4] but the parallels to the neoliberal transformation that occurred in the last decades of the twentieth century are apparent. Polanyi warned against the commodification of labour, land and money that, if left unchecked, would ultimately destroy society. As the American sociologist Michael Burawoy has put it:

> When labor power is exchanged without protection against injury or sickness, unemployment or over-employment, or below-subsistence wages, the labor that can be extracted rapidly declines, and it veers towards uselessness. Equally, when land, or more broadly nature, is subject to commodification then it can no longer support the basic necessities for human life. Finally, when money is used to make money, for example through currency speculation, then its value becomes so uncertain that it can no longer be used as a means of exchange, putting businesses out of business and generating economic crises.[5]

In his analysis, Polanyi focused on a number of specific forms that counter-movements mobilizing people who feel betrayed by changes such as those produced by neoliberalism can be expected to take. Such counter-movements, he claimed, are in fact reactive movements – that is, their stance is defensive and backward-looking. Indeed, they are often established in order to resist an ideology that preaches the dominance of the market over every other aspect of society. To give just two examples: in many cases, peasant rebellions broke out when peasants felt an implicit social contract offering them at least minimal protection against the whims of the market had been violated. Similarly, food riots have often been interpreted as reactions to the destruction of a moral economy, in the course of which common lands are enclosed and the markets for basic goods, such as bread, are deregulated. History teaches us that counter-movements seeking the re-establishment of traditionally guaranteed rights can put forward progressive narratives and offer more inclusive and participatory visions, but they can also draw on regressive models and exclusive and plebiscitary ideas.

The political implementation of neoliberal economic dogmas has revealed certain parallels to the 'Great Transformation' as described by Polanyi. After successful resistance to rampant market fundamentalism had brought about an expansion of social protections within nation-states (including the social democracies of the so-called 'First World' and the 'actually existing socialism' of the 'Second World'), a general retrenchment of the welfare state and a broader attack against state interventions targeting social inequality became dominant trends. With the neoliberal turn, capitalism once again began to rely (albeit in different ways) on forms of accumulation by dispossession – for example by repealing laws that protected citizens' rights and regulated the financial markets – that Marx once identified as typical forms of what he called 'primitive accumulation'.[6] The commodification of labour, land and money was again pursued through the deregulation of labour markets and the dismantling of worker protections, land-grabbing, and a new (and comprehensive) deregulation of financial capital.

Once again, counter-forces (similar to what Polanyi had called counter-movements) emerged, developing in two directions: some are progressive, seeking to expand citizens' rights within an inclusive, cosmopolitan conception; others are regressive, yearning for a bygone order in which only a restricted number of insiders were protected. Before attending to the question of how reactionary counter-movements against neoliberalism can emerge, let me begin with a couple of observations regarding the progressive variant.

Progressive movements against neoliberal globalization

The anti-austerity protests of 2011–14 were reacting to a sense of political dispossession in the context of a separation between popular politics and institutional power. They focused on domestic conditions, although they were aware of the global entanglements of the respective nations in which the protests occurred. Beginning with the Icelandic 'pots and pans' revolt of 2008, and again during the Arab Spring and the Occupy movement of 2011 and the Gezi Park protests of 2013, the need to hold together a heterogeneous social base – as well as the general failure of established ideologies to provide attractive alternative visions of social and political organization – fuelled the development of pluralist and tolerant identities, exulting in diversity as an enriching value. This was reflected at the organizational level through the elaboration of a participatory and deliberative model of decision making.[7] However, the crisis of neoliberalism also had an impact on contemporary progressive politics. When the later movements are compared to the first wave of protests against rampant neoliberalism in 1999 and after, we can detect a change in terms of the social base, a renewed focus on the defence of traditional rights guaranteed within a national context, and an emphasis on moral protection against an immoral capitalism.

Sometimes referred to as the 'precariat', those protesting austerity represented coalitions of various classes and social groups who perceived themselves as the losers of neoliberal policies. Precariousness was certainly a social and cultural condition for many movement activists, a majority of whom belonged to a generation characterized by high levels of unemployment and under-employment. The most marginalized sections of the young took the lead in the Arab Spring, and those affected by the financial crisis mobilized in various forms across Southern Europe (in Portugal they define themselves as a generation 'without a future'). These young people are not those traditionally thought of as losers. Rather, they are the well-educated and the mobile, once described as globalization's 'winners', but far from enjoying such a self-perception today.

That said, the well-educated youth are not the only social group set to lose out in the neoliberal assault on civil and social rights. Take, for example, two groups that were once considered especially well protected: retirees and public employees. To a greater or lesser extent, their life conditions (including access to fundamental goods such as healthcare, housing and education) have become increasingly precarious. Similarly, blue-collar workers in small and large factories alike, whether already closed or in danger of being closed, also participated in the wave of protests. With high levels of participation among young people and well-educated citizens, the demonstrations brought into the streets a sort of (inverted) '2/3' society of those most affected by austerity policies.[8]

As Zygmunt Bauman has authoritatively shown,[9] neoliberalism produces a liquid society that destroys the old bases for personal, collective and political identity through forced mobility and related insecurity. As such, identification processes are strongly reshaped by the changing culture of neoliberalism and once again assume a central role. While the labour movement developed a distinct identity supported by a complex ideology, and the new social movements cultivated a focus on specific concerns such as gender rights or the defence of the environment, the identification processes of the anti-austerity protestors seemed to challenge individualization as well as its fear and exclusivism, calling instead for inclusive citizenship. Defining themselves broadly – as citizens, persons, or the 99 per cent – they developed a moral discourse calling for the reinstatement of welfare protections but also (indignantly) challenging the injustice of the system as a whole.

Often referring to the nation as the basis of a community of solidarity (by, for example, carrying national flags or, in the case of Podemos, appealing to *la patria*, the fatherland), they nevertheless developed a cosmopolitan vision that combined inclusive nationalism with the recognition of the need to find global solutions to global problems. A strong moral framing also grew to challenge the perceived amorality of neoliberalism and its ideological propagation of the commodification of public services. The cynical, neoliberal view that individuals are personally responsible for their own survival and that selfish motives are socially beneficial was stigmatized in the name of previously existing rights and coupled with demands for their re-establishment. A call for solidarity and a return to the commons was pitted against neoliberal policies which were perceived as unjust and inefficient.

As the economic crisis was accompanied by a crisis of political legitimacy, more and more groups in society ceased to feel represented within institutions that were increasingly viewed as being firmly in the hands of big business. The critique of the collusion between economic and political power grew louder.[10] Today, protestors actively criticize the power of big corporations and unaccountable international organizations, together with the related loss of national governmental sovereignty. Moreover, they hold their respective governments and the political class at large responsible for what they perceive to be an abduction of democracy. However, rather than developing anti-democratic attitudes, they call for participatory democracy and a general return to public concern with common goods. In contrast to the global justice movement, which presented itself as an alliance of minorities in search of a wider constituency,[11] the anti-austerity movements have constructed a broad definition of their collective identities as encompassing the majority of citizens.

In this situation, the claims voiced during the anti-austerity protests have been oriented especially towards the defence of rights won in 'First World' democracies in the 1960s and 1970s, but also in 'Second World' socialist states and 'Third World' developing countries.[12] While characterized by a focus on national sovereignty and resistance to the dispossession of citizens' rights by electorally unaccountable global elites, the anti-austerity protests of 2011–14 nevertheless defended political and social rights as *human rights*. The denunciation of the corruption of the 1 per cent (and, accordingly, the defence of the 99 per cent) was framed as a struggle against the centralization of economic and political power in the hands of a small oligarchy. In a sense, the anti-austerity protests were backward-looking, in that they called for the restoration of lost rights and vehemently denounced the corruption of democracy. However, they also looked forward, combining concerns for social rights with hopes for cultural inclusivity.

Given the extremely low level of trust in existing representative institutions, these movements have addressed demands to the state, while also experimenting with alternative models of participatory and deliberative democracy. In Spain, the *acampadas*, the camps originally set up by demonstrators in Madrid's Puerta del Sol, became places to experiment with new forms of democracy. However, it was not democracy per se that was being challenged, but rather its degeneration – as the poster of one *indignado* read: Lo llaman democracia y no lo es ('They call it democracy, but it is not'). Demanding, as in Spain in 2011, *real* democracy ('¡Democracia real ya!'), activists proposed a different – deliberative and participatory – vision of democracy, and developed their own organizational forms in the process. As neoliberalism attacked the corporatist actors that had driven the social pacts of Fordist capitalism – first the unions, but also the many civil society organizations integrated into the provision of social protection – the emerging movements began to cherish the idea of a direct democracy driven by the citizens themselves.

While contingently less visible, this progressive side of social movements is alive and well. Particularly in Southern Europe, the political effects of their protests are reflected in a broad politicization of society in general as well as deep changes in the party systems, with broader representation of the movements' concerns now found in their respective parliaments (from Podemos in Spain to Bloco de Esquerda in Portugal and the Movimento 5 Stelle in Italy), or even in the government itself (with Syriza in Greece).[13] Even in the UK and the United States, the two countries where the reactionary populist turn has been felt most sharply, the Occupy protests have left their marks on party politics: Jeremy Corbyn was elected leader of the Labour Party, and Bernie Sanders was remarkably successful in the Democratic primaries.

Nevertheless, in the public debate, these progressive movements on the left have been temporarily eclipsed by the success of right-wing parties.

Regressive movements?

The impression that we are witnessing a 'Great Regression' has been fuelled by events culminating in the Brexit vote and Trump's presidential victory, but it is also reinforced by developments in France, where the Front National has a long history, in Germany by the rapid growth of Alternative für Deutschland, as well as in Austria, the Scandinavian countries, Poland and Hungary. The Tea Party in the US, Pegida in Germany, the English Defence League in the UK, the Bloc identitaire in France and CasaPound in Italy have all emerged as examples of right-wing politics in the form of social movements. While there is still too little empirical evidence to develop an elaborate analysis of this regressive shift, we can at least begin to frame some of the relevant questions. Firstly, we must address the social basis of discontent under neoliberalism that has fuelled the political right's transformation.

Social and political scientists claim to have identified a new cleavage that has emerged as a consequence of globalization, one that separates the winners (those who have an exit option) from the losers (those lacking such an option):

> The likely winners of globalization include entrepreneurs and qualified employees in sectors open to international competition, as well as cosmopolitan citizens. Losers of globalization, by contrast, include entrepreneurs and qualified employees in traditionally protected sectors, all unqualified employees, and citizens who strongly identify themselves with their national community.[14]

Initial data on Brexit and the US presidential elections indicate, however, that blue-collar workers and members of the downwardly mobile middle class were not the only (or even primary) supporters of the 'Leave' campaign and Donald Trump. There was strong support among the rich and highly educated as well. Money played a crucial role in these right-wing victories: big business and well-funded think-tanks first supported the Tea Party and later the Trump campaign. Money was injected into media campaigns spreading simple messages, often blatantly untrue, that appealed to fear and directed public outrage towards various scapegoats while mobilizing the traditional conservative basis of the Republican Party. Though not the whole story, this is an important element thereof that should not be forgotten. As in the past, regressive counter-movements pretend to express solidarity with the 99 per cent while still enjoying the support of the powerful 1 per cent (as the stock markets' positive reaction to Trump's victory clearly demonstrates).

A second question addresses the forms that this discontent takes on the right. They appear to be very different from those on the left, not only with respect to the sociopolitical content of their claims, but also with regard to organizational models. Research on right-wing populism has long identified a cultural demarcation – with cosmopolitanism on the one side and xenophobia on the other – that separates the political left from the right.[15] This is all the more apparent today. Additionally, politics on the right is characterized by a specific organizational form that builds on strong, personalized leadership rather than citizen participation. This clearly differentiates it from progressive movements.

Because of their appeal to the will of the people, as opposed to pandering to corrupt elites, recent progressive movements have also been defined as populist. However, this understanding of populism seems to be too 'thin' – after all, what political party or movement does not appeal to the people? Instead, we should adopt a different conceptualization of populism, one that defines it as a form of popular subjectivity. As the political scientist Kenneth Roberts has noted, whereas social movements 'emerge from autonomous forms of collective action undertaken by self-constituted civic groups or networks, populism typically involves an appropriation of popular subjectivity by dominant personalities who control the channels, rhythms, and organizational forms of social mobilization'. His definition of populism aptly describes phenomena such as Trump's electoral campaign:

> populism does not require that mass constituencies engage in collective action at all, beyond the individual act of casting a ballot in national elections or popular referendums. Although both forms of popular subjectivity contest established elites, social movements mobilize such contestation from the bottom-up, whereas populism typically mobilizes mass constituencies from the top-down behind the leadership of a counter-elite.[16]

The contrast between social movements on the one hand and populism on the other is especially strong when it comes to plebiscitary versus participatory relations between the people and the leaders:

> These linkages ultimately embody very different forms of popular subjectivity and collective action. Participatory linkages or patterns of subjectivity provide citizens with a direct role in contesting established elites or in deliberative and policy-making processes. As such, they tend to rely on autonomous and self-constituted forms of collective action at the grass-roots, inside or out of (and sometimes against) formal institutional channels. By contrast, under plebiscitary linkages or patterns of subjectivity, mass constituencies – often unorganized – are mobilized from above to acclaim an authority figure or ratify their leader's political initiatives. Such plebiscitary

acclamation often resides in the voting booth or popular referendums, and is not predicated on autonomous forms of collective action at the grass-roots. Indeed, plebiscitary appeals often rest on a direct, unmediated relationship between a populist figure and highly fragmented mass constituencies.[17]

Although both types of subjectivity invoke 'the people' and stigmatize elites, populism is tied to a plebiscitary linkage which does not empower the people as a whole, but rather an individual leader. This plebiscitarian turn can be seen in regressive politics, with leaders appealing to the masses through anti-establishment discourses while manipulating rather than involving 'the people'.

Thirdly, the question of under which political conditions a regressive counter-movement can develop remains to be addressed. In general, scholars who study social movements have looked at political opportunities and threats as affecting the extent and characteristics of protest. Research on progressive movements has clearly shown that the specific characteristics of the contemporary discontent with neoliberalism and its crisis are influenced by the political responses to the great recession, and by the strategies of centre-left (especially party) politics in particular. Notably, research on anti-austerity protests in Latin America has shown that the most destabilizing waves occurred where party politics failed to offer channels of anti-neoliberal dissent, as all major parties supported neoliberal policies.[18] A similar situation seems to be emerging in Europe, where the consequences of a repositioning on the right in terms of (exclusive) visions of social protection seem all the more dramatic when the left is perceived as championing free markets and lacking a significant alternative.[19]

On movements and counter-movements: some conclusions

Discontent with neoliberalism and its crisis comes in different political forms. On the left, protests have often taken the organizational form of networked social movements, whereas on the right new parties have emerged and others have been transformed through the development of a plebiscitary linkage between leaders and followers. As was often the case historically, sources of discontent are framed on the left within a discourse of cosmopolitanism and class. On the right, however, the same discontent is mostly positioned within exclusive and xenophobic discourses. This does not mean that regressive movements are necessarily more successful, but rather that – as has happened in the past, especially in times of economic crisis – left-wing advances are resisted by powerful actors (as when labour movement victories are followed by reactionary rollbacks).

While progressive politics remains alive and well, the right's recent visible successes point to the challenges that the current situation poses for the left. First, the fragmentation of the social base is certainly a problem for progressive politics, as expressions of discontent can be expected to follow different logics simultaneously – struggling against commodification (as in the most traditional labour conflicts), but also against re-commodification (in the form of privatization of goods and services) and ex-commodification (the expulsion of actors from the market through massive unemployment and the precarization of labour).[20]

At the same time, and even more so than in the previous wave of progressive politics during the heyday of the global justice movement, there is an urgent need on the left for transnational coordination which may potentially weaken previously cultivated mobilization structures. Local resistance to the eradication of existing rights may very well clash with the need for global efforts to harness globalized financial capitalism.

Finally, progressive activists and voters – who typically hold strong normative beliefs and are accustomed to a sophisticated level of discourse – are more difficult to win over with generic appeals or outright lies. They are therefore increasingly difficult to mobilize through the neoliberal appeals of the centre left, which has indeed been the big political loser in recent developments. At the same time, while the radical left has grown stronger and stronger, especially where progressive social movements have been most widespread, only on rare occasions have movement parties been able to attain decision-making power in national institutions. Where they have done so, as in Bolivia and Greece, they encounter enormous resistance both inside and outside their respective countries.

Addressing these challenges doubtless requires patience, but it also requires the creation of spaces for encounters and learning in action, through the practice of struggle, as was also the case with progressive movements in the past.

Notes

1 Donatella della Porta, *Social Movements in Times of Austerity*, Cambridge: Polity, 2015.
2 Hanspeter Kriesi et al., *West European Politics in the Age of Globalization*, Cambridge: Cambridge University Press, 2008.
3 Manuela Caiani, Donatella della Porta and Claudius Wagemann, *Mobilizing on the Extreme Right: Germany, Italy and the United States*, Oxford: Oxford University Press, 2012.
4 Karl Polanyi, *The Great Transformation: The Political and Economic Origins of Our Time*, London: Beacon Press, 1957.
5 Michael Burawoy, 'Facing an Unequal World', *Current Sociology*, 63:1 (2015), p. 19.
6 See, among others, David Harvey, *A Brief History of Neoliberalism*, Oxford: Oxford University Press, 2005.
7 Donatella della Porta, *Can Democracy be Saved?*, Oxford: Polity, 2013; della Porta, *Social Movements in Times of Austerity*.
8 Della Porta, *Social Movements in Times of Austerity*.
9 Zygmunt Bauman, *Liquid Modernity*, Oxford: Polity, 2000.
10 Colin Crouch, *The Strange Non-Death of Neoliberalism*, Oxford: Polity, 2012.
11 Donatella della Porta, *Democracy in Social Movements*, London: Palgrave, 2009; della Porta (ed.), *Another Europe: Conceptions and Practices of Democracy in the European Social Forums*, London: Routledge, 2009.
12 Donatella della Porta et al., *Late Neoliberalism and its Discontents in the Economic Crisis*, London: Palgrave, forthcoming.
13 Donatella della Porta, *The Global Spreading of Protest*, Amsterdam: Amsterdam University Press, forthcoming; della Porta, Joseba Fernández, Hara Kouki and Lorenzo Mosca, *Movement Parties Against Austerity*, Cambridge: Polity, forthcoming.
14 Kriesi et al., *West European Politics in the Age of Globalization*, p. 8.
15 Ibid.
16 Kenneth Roberts, 'Populism and Social Movements', in Donatella della Porta and Mario Diani (eds), *Oxford Handbook on*

Social Movements, Oxford: Oxford University Press, 2015, pp. 681–2.

17 Ibid., p. 685.

18 Kenneth Roberts, *Changing Course in Latin America: Party Systems in the Neoliberal Era*, Cambridge: Cambridge University Press, 2015.

19 See della Porta, *The Global Spreading of Protest*.

20 See Burawoy, 'Facing an Unequal World'.

4

Progressive neoliberalism versus reactionary populism: a Hobson's choice

Nancy Fraser

The election of Donald Trump represents one in a series of dramatic political uprisings that together signal a collapse of neoliberal hegemony. These uprisings include the Brexit vote in the United Kingdom, the rejection of the Renzi reforms in Italy, Bernie Sanders' campaign for the Democratic Party nomination in the United States, and rising support for the National Front in France, among others. Although they differ in ideologies and goals, these electoral mutinies share a common target: all are rejections of corporate globalization, neoliberalism and the political establishments that have promoted them. In every case, voters are saying 'No!' to the lethal combination of austerity, free trade, predatory debt and precarious, ill-paid work that characterizes present-day financialized capitalism. Their votes represent the subjective political counterpart to the objective structural crisis of this form of capitalism. Manifest for some time in the 'slow violence' associated with global warming and the worldwide assault on social reproduction, this structural crisis erupted into full view in 2007–8 with the near meltdown of global financial order.

Until recently, however, the chief response to the crisis was *social* protest – dramatic and lively, to be sure, but largely ephemeral. *Political* systems, by contrast, seemed relatively immune, still controlled by party functionaries and establishment elites, at least in the most powerful states of the capitalist core, such as the United States, the United Kingdom and Germany. Now, however, electoral shock waves reverberate throughout the world, including in the citadels of global finance. Those who voted for Trump, like those who voted for Brexit and against the Italian reforms, have risen up against their political masters. Thumbing their noses at party establishments, they have repudiated the arrangements that have been hollowing out their living conditions for the last thirty years. The surprise is not that they have done so, but that it took them so long.

Nevertheless, Trump's victory is not solely a revolt against global finance. What his voters rejected was not neoliberalism tout court, but *progressive* neoliberalism. This may sound to some like an oxymoron, but it is a real, if perverse, political alignment that holds the key to understanding the US election results – and perhaps some developments elsewhere as well. In its US form, progressive neoliberalism is an alliance of mainstream currents of new social movements (feminism, anti-racism, multiculturalism and LGBTQ rights) on the one side, and high-end 'symbolic' and service-based sectors of business (Wall Street, Silicon Valley and Hollywood) on the other. In this alliance, progressive forces are effectively joined with the forces of cognitive capitalism, especially financialization. However unwittingly, the former lend their charisma to the latter. Ideals like diversity and empowerment, which could in principle serve different ends, now gloss policies that have devastated manufacturing and the middle-class livelihoods that were once available to those engaged in it.

Progressive neoliberalism developed in the United States roughly over the last three decades and was ratified with Bill Clinton's election in 1992. Clinton was the principal engineer and standard-bearer of the 'New Democrats', the US equivalent of Tony Blair's New Labour. In place of the New Deal coalition of unionized manufacturing workers, African-Americans and the urban middle classes, he forged a new alliance of entrepreneurs, suburbanites, new social movements and youth, all proclaiming their modern, progressive bona fides by embracing diversity, multiculturalism and women's rights. Even as it endorsed such progressive notions, the Clinton administration courted Wall Street. Turning the US economy over to Goldman Sachs, it deregulated the banking system and negotiated the free-trade agreements that accelerated deindustrialization. What fell by the wayside was the Rustbelt – once the stronghold of New Deal social democracy, and now the region that delivered the Electoral College to Donald Trump. That region, along with newer industrial centres in the South, took a major hit as runaway financialization unfolded over the course of the last two decades. Continued by his successors, including Barack Obama, Clinton's policies degraded the living conditions of all working people, but especially those employed in industrial production. In short, Clintonism bears a heavy share of responsibility for the weakening of unions, the decline of real wages, the increasing precarity of work, and the rise of the 'two-earner family' in place of the defunct family wage.

As that last point suggests, the assault on social security was glossed by a veneer of emancipatory charisma, borrowed from the new social movements. Though presented as a feminist triumph, the reality beneath the ideal of the two-earner family is depressed wage levels, decreased job security, declining living standards, a steep rise in the number of hours worked for wages per household, exacerbation of the double shift (now often a triple or quadruple shift), a rise in female-headed households, and a desperate struggle to shift care work onto others, especially onto poor, racialized and/or immigrant women. Throughout the years when manufacturing cratered, moreover, the US buzzed with talk of 'diversity', 'women's empowerment' and 'the battle against discrimination'. Identifying progress with meritocracy as opposed to equality, these terms equated emancipation with the rise of 'talented' women, minorities and gays in the winner-takes-all corporate hierarchy, instead of with the latter's abolition. These liberal-individualist views of progress gradually replaced the more expansive, anti-hierarchical, egalitarian, class-sensitive and anti-capitalist understandings of emancipation that had flourished in the 1960s and 1970s. As the New Left waned, its structural critique of capitalist society faded, and the country's characteristic liberal-individualist mindset reasserted itself, imperceptibly shrinking the aspirations of 'progressives' and self-proclaimed leftists. What sealed the deal, however, was the coincidence of this evolution with the rise of neoliberalism. A party bent on liberalizing the capitalist economy found its perfect mate in a meritocratic corporate feminism focused on 'leaning in' and 'cracking the glass ceiling'.

What lay behind these developments was an epochal transformation of capitalism that began in the 1970s and is now unravelling. The structural aspect of that transformation is well understood: whereas the previous regime of state-managed capitalism empowered governments to subordinate the short-term interests of private firms to the long-term objective of sustained accumulation, the current one authorizes global finance to discipline governments and populations in the immediate interests of private investors. But the political aspect is less well understood. We might characterize it in terms adapted from Karl Polanyi. Combining mass production and mass consumption with public provision, state-managed capitalism creatively synthesized two projects that Polanyi considered antithetical: marketization and social protection. But they teamed up at the expense of a third project, neglected by him, which can be called emancipation, in so far as the whole edifice rested on the ongoing (neo-)imperial predation of the Global South, on the institutionalization of women's dependency through the family wage, and on the racially motivated exclusion of agricultural and domestic workers from social security. By the 1960s those excluded populations were actively mobilizing against a bargain that required them to pay the price of others' relative security and prosperity. And rightly so! But their struggles intersected fatefully with another front of struggle, which unfolded in parallel over the course of the subsequent decades. That second front pitted an ascending party of free-marketeers, bent on liberalizing and globalizing the capitalist economy, against declining labour movements in the countries of the capitalist core, once the most powerful base of support for social democracy, but now on the defensive, if not wholly defeated. In this context progressive new social movements, aiming to overturn hierarchies of gender, 'race'-ethnicity and sex, found themselves pitted against populations seeking to defend established lifeworlds and privileges, now threatened by the cosmopolitanism of the new financialized economy. The collision of these two fronts of struggle produced a new constellation: *proponents of emancipation joined up with partisans of financialization to double-team social protection.* The fruit of their union was progressive neoliberalism.

Progressive neoliberalism mixes together truncated ideals of emancipation and lethal forms of financialization. It was precisely that mix that was rejected *in toto* by Trump's voters. Prominent among those left behind in this brave new cosmopolitan world are industrial workers, to be sure, but also managers, small businessmen, and all who relied on industry in the Rust Belt and the South, as well as rural populations devastated by unemployment and drugs. For these populations, the injury of deindustrialization is compounded by the insult of progressive moralism, which routinely portrays them as culturally backward. Rejecting globalization, Trump voters also repudiated the liberal cosmopolitanism identified with it. For some (though by no means all), it was a short step to blaming their worsening conditions on political correctness, people of colour, immigrants and Muslims. In their eyes, feminism and Wall Street are birds of a feather, perfectly united in the person of Hillary Clinton.

What made possible that conflation was the absence of any genuine left. Despite periodic outbursts such as Occupy Wall Street, which proved short-lived, there had been no sustained left presence in the United States for several decades. Nor was there in place any comprehensive left narrative that articulated the legitimate grievances of Trump supporters with a fulsome critique of financialization, on the one hand, and with an anti-racist, anti-sexist and anti-hierarchical vision of emancipation, on the other. Equally devastating, potential links between labour and new social movements were left to languish. Split off from one another, those indispensable poles of a viable left were miles apart, waiting to be counterposed as antithetical.

At least until the remarkable primary campaign of Bernie Sanders, who struggled to unite those two poles after some prodding from Black Lives Matter. Exploding the reigning neoliberal common sense, Sanders campaigned against 'the rigged economy', which has been redistributing wealth and income upward on a massive scale for the last thirty years. He also targeted 'the rigged political system' that has supported and protected that economy, as Democrats and Republicans have conspired for decades to squelch every serious proposal for structural reform, even as their other battles saturated the public sphere and sucked up all the oxygen there. Flying the banner of 'democratic socialism', Sanders forged sentiments that had lain dormant since Occupy Wall Street into a powerful political insurgency.

Sanders' revolt was the parallel on the Democratic side to that of Trump. Even as the latter was upending the Republican establishment, Bernie came within a hair's breadth of defeating Obama's anointed successor, whose apparatchiks controlled every lever of power in the Democratic Party. Between them, Sanders and Trump galvanized a huge majority of American voters. But only Trump's populism survived. While he easily routed his Republican rivals, including those favoured by the big donors and party bosses, the Sanders insurrection was effectively checked by a far less democratic Democratic Party. By the time of the general election, then, the left alternative had been suppressed.

What remained was the Hobson's choice between reactionary populism and progressive neoliberalism. Pivoting quickly to small-bore moralizing, Hillary Clinton centred her entire campaign on Trump's 'badness'. It was true, of course, that he was the gift that kept on giving, serving up an unending series of provocations, each more noxious than the last, and providing an inexhaustible supply of pretexts for evading the issues that Sanders had raised. But Clinton played true to type and took the bait. Zeroing in on Trump's insults to Muslims and his groping of women, and taking for granted Sanders' supporters, she dropped all references to the 'rigged economy', the need for a 'political revolution', the social costs of neoliberal free trade and financialization, and the extreme maldistribution of those costs. Nor did she accord any legitimacy to Trump's dissident views of US foreign policy, including his doubts about serial regime change, the future of NATO and the demonization of Russia. Convinced that a candidate of her qualifications could not possibly lose to a man as wild and unprepared as Donald Trump, Clinton assumed that all she needed to do was whip up moral outrage and run out the clock. Trotting out the usual scare tactics, her surrogates turned up the heat on Sanders' supporters. To stop the 'fascist' threat, they needed to cease their criticisms of the candidate and dutifully get behind the lesser evil.

But that strategy proved disastrous – and not just because Clinton lost. By failing to address the conditions that had enabled the rise of Trump, her campaign simply wrote off his supporters and their concerns. The effect was to cement the perception of progressives as allies of global finance – a view buttressed by the release of Clinton's speeches to Goldman Sachs. Far from 'pushing her to the left', as some reluctant supporters hoped to do, they only reinforced the stark choice between two unpalatable alternatives: reactionary populism or progressive neoliberalism.

In fact, such 'lesser evil-ism' was hardly new. This was the US left's habitual posture, dusted off every four years: ventriloquizing liberal objectives and squelching its own, out of fear of a Bush or a Trump. Although aimed at saving us from 'the worst', that strategy actually fertilizes the soil that germinates new and ever more dangerous bogeymen, which in turn justify further deferments – and on and on, in a vicious circle. Does anyone believe that a Clinton presidency would have gone after Wall Street and the 1 per cent? That it would have diminished rather than stoked populist rage? In fact, the rage felt by many Trump supporters is quite legitimate, even if much of it is currently mal-directed towards immigrants and other scapegoats. The proper response is not moral condemnation but political validation, while redirecting the rage to the systemic predations of finance capital.

That response also serves to answer those who urge that we now close ranks with the neoliberals to ward off fascism. The problem is not only that reactionary populism is not (yet) fascism. It is also that, seen analytically, liberalism and fascism are not really two separate things, one of which is good and the other bad, but two deeply interconnected faces of the capitalist world system. Although they are by no means normatively equivalent, both are products of unrestrained capitalism, which everywhere destabilizes lifeworlds and habitats, bringing in its wake both individual liberation and untold suffering. Liberalism expresses the first, liberatory side of this process, while glossing over the rage and pain associated with the second. Left to fester in the absence of an alternative, those sentiments fuel authoritarianisms

of every sort, including those that really deserve the name
fascism and those that emphatically do not. Without a left,
in other words, the maelstrom of capitalist 'development'
can only generate liberal forces and authoritarian counter-
forces, bound together in a perverse symbiosis. Thus, far
from being the antidote to fascism, (neo)liberalism is its
partner in crime. The real charm against fascism (whether
proto or quasi or real) is a left project that redirects the rage
and the pain of the dispossessed towards a deep societal
restructuring and a democratic political 'revolution'. Until
very recently, such a project could not even be glimpsed, so
suffocatingly hegemonic was neoliberal common sense. But
thanks to Sanders, Corbyn, Syriza, Podemos – imperfect as
all of them are – we can again envision an expanded set of
possibilities.

From here on out, accordingly: *the left should refuse the
choice between progressive neoliberalism and reactionary
populism*. Rather than accepting the terms presented to us
by the political classes, we should be working to redefine
them by drawing on the vast and growing fund of social
revulsion against the present order. Rather than siding with
financialization-cum-emancipation against social protection,
we should be focused on forging a new alliance of emancipation and social protection against financialization. In this
project, which builds on that of Sanders, emancipation does
not mean diversifying corporate hierarchy, but rather abolishing it. And prosperity does not mean rising share value or
corporate profit, but the material prerequisites of a good life
for all. This combination remains the only principled and
winning response in the current conjuncture.

I, for one, shed no tears for the defeat of progressive
neoliberalism. Certainly there is much to fear from a racist,
anti-immigrant and anti-ecological Trump administration.
But we should mourn neither the implosion of neoliberal
hegemony nor the shattering of Clintonism's iron grip on the
Democratic Party. Trump's victory marked a defeat for the
unholy alliance of emancipation with financialization. But
his presidency offers no resolution of the present crisis, no
promise of a new regime, no secure hegemony. What we face,
rather, is an interregnum, an open and unstable situation in
which hearts and minds are up for grabs. In this situation,

there is not only danger but also opportunity: the chance to build a new 'new left'.

Whether that happens will depend in part on some serious soul-searching among the progressives who rallied to the Clinton campaign. They will need to drop the comforting but false myth that they lost to a 'basket of deplorables' (racists, misogynists, Islamophobes and homophobes) aided by Vladimir Putin and the FBI. They will need to acknowledge their own share of blame for sacrificing the cause of social protection, material well-being and working-class dignity to faux understandings of emancipation in terms of meritocracy, diversity and empowerment. They will need to think deeply about how we might transform the political economy of financialized capitalism, reviving Sanders' watchword of 'democratic socialism' and figuring out what it might mean in the twenty-first century. They will need, above all, to reach out to the mass of Trump voters who are neither racists nor committed right-wingers, but casualties of a 'rigged system' who can and must be recruited to the anti-neoliberal project of a rejuvenated left.

This does *not* mean muting pressing concerns about racism or sexism. But it does mean showing how those long-standing historical oppressions find new expressions and grounds today, in financialized capitalism. Rebutting the false, zero-sum thinking that dominated the election campaign, we should link the harms suffered by women and people of colour to those experienced by the many who voted for Trump. In that way, a revitalized left could lay the foundation for a powerful new coalition committed to fighting for justice for all.

5

From the paradox of liberation to the demise of liberal elites

Eva Illouz

The world seems to have become, almost overnight, disorganized. Within liberal, democratic societies we can observe a radicalization of populations which since the Second World War had, by and large, accepted and followed the rules of the liberal game. Whether in the United States, France, Great Britain, Austria, Germany, Hungary or Israel, a significant section of the people seems now intent on questioning some of the key motives of liberalism: religious and ethnic pluralism, integration of the nation into a world order through economic exchange and global institutions, expansion of individual and group rights, tolerance of sexual diversity, religious and ethnic neutrality of the state. Outside the traditional Western liberal world the situation is even bleaker: Russia, Turkey and the Philippines show a style of aggressive, brutal, chauvinistic leadership, and a disinhibited disregard for the rule of law and human rights.

We used to think of fundamentalism as that feature of thought and action that characterizes the 'other' of the West, and, in that vein, much has been written about Islamist fundamentalism as the other. Yet, ironically, the most palpably proximate 'other' to have emerged is the one from within our midst. I will focus here on this proximate fundamentalism, that of populations who live in Western or Western-aspiring democracies and which seem to be motivated by a desire to return to the 'fundaments' of their culture, civilization, religion and nation, all in one. This fundamentalism is fuelled by religion and tradition, to be sure, but religion is essentially mobilized to defend the purity of the people and a radical version of the nation.

In this essay, for the most part, I consider this process of internal radicalization from a tiny corner of the globe, that of Israel. Israel is interesting for a discussion of the general disorder inasmuch as it shifted to regressive populist politics at least one decade before the global slide into populism we are now witnessing (what Christophe Ayad has called the 'Israelisation of the world').[1] This reactionary Israeli politics is manifest in a number of ways: in the radicalization of the reigning Likud Party (especially following the 2009 elections) and its shift to an alt-right politics, with the overt aim of establishing Jewish supremacy over the Arabs (with a prominent Likud Member of the Knesset recently saying that he would prefer if Arab citizens stopped exercising their right to vote); in the mainstreaming of extreme messianic politicians calling for the restoration of a Great Biblical Israel (a position that was viewed as sheer lunacy only a decade ago); in the public delegitimation of left-wing opinions, now dubbed by many state officials as acts of 'treason' (in some cases, they have been made illegal altogether, as for example with the call to support the Boycott, Divestment and Sanctions Movement, BDS); in the incessant invocation of security to justify violations of privacy and minority rights; and with rabbis on the public payroll calling for a refusal to employ Arabs and for boycotting shops that do so. A recent survey conducted among Israeli Jewish youth in grades 11 and 12 by *Israel Hayom*, a daily paper owned by Sheldon Adelson (the Jewish billionaire who has contributed millions of dollars to both Netanyahu *and* Trump), captures these deep trends: 59 per cent identified as politically right-wing, and only 13 per cent said they considered themselves left-wing. The survey also revealed a surprisingly high level of patriotism, with 85 per cent saying they 'love the country', and 65 per cent saying they agreed with the adage attributed to Zionist hero Joseph Trumpeldor, who was killed in battle in 1920: 'It is good to die for one's country.'[2]

The shift from what was a presumably liberal country to a populist one (characterized by a disregard for international law and the civic values of liberalism) has been attributed to the failure of the accords of Oslo, Wye and Camp David, after which the Palestinians were accused of rejecting the territorial offers made by the left-wing government of Ehud Barak. This undoubtedly played an important role in making the securitist rhetoric of the right both more strident and more acceptable, but it alone cannot explain the palpable change of political identity of Israel, its shift in civic culture and values.

To understand what might be at stake in these changes, I will begin my discussion with Michael Walzer's recent book *The Paradox of Liberation*, which examines the process of internal radicalization of three nations: Algeria, Israel and India. The question at the centre of the book is: how is it that in all three countries, whose independence had been recently snatched out of the hands of colonial powers, the movement that liberated people was so quickly challenged by religious fundamentalists and was so weak in answering them? I do not refer to Walzer's thesis here because I endorse it. On the contrary: Walzer is one of the most prominent political philosophers of our times, and his understanding of 'what went wrong' is important not only because of the eminence of the author, but also because it contains glaring diagnostic errors.

Paradoxes of liberation

In this section, I will follow Walzer's argument closely, merely paraphrasing him. The puzzle at the centre of his book is this: in 'three different countries, with three different religions, the timetable was remarkably similar: roughly twenty to thirty years after independence, the secular state was challenged by a militant religious movement'.[3] The paradox described by Walzer is that the liberationists were at war with the people they wanted to liberate, because they were secular while the people were (or increasingly became) religious.

Walzer quotes the writer V. S. Naipaul, who invokes the Indian case – but where Naipaul writes 'Hinduism' one can easily read 'Diaspora Judaism', as viewed by early Zionists:

Hinduism ... has exposed us to a thousand years of defeat and stagnation. It has given men no idea of a contract with

other men, no idea of a state. It has enslaved one quarter of
the population and always left the whole fragmented and
vulnerable. Its philosophy of withdrawal has diminished men
intellectually and not equipped them to respond to challenge;
it has stifled growth.[4]

National liberation, by contrast, is a secularizing, modernizing and developmental creed – precisely the creed that is
now challenged everywhere around the globe. It is, as its
opponents say, a 'Western' creed, and to the nation about to
be liberated it is something entirely new. Indeed, newness is
the mantra of the liberators. They offer the oppressed people
the vision and promises of new beginnings, new politics, a
new culture, a new economy; they aim to create new men and
women. Walzer quotes David Ben-Gurion, the first and most
long-lasting prime minister of Israel: 'The worker of Eretz
Yisrael [the Land of Israel] differs from the Jewish worker in
Galut [exile] … [He is] not a new branch grafted to an old
tradition, but a new tree.'[5]
    And yet, in 'all three countries religion remained a force
in everyday life during the years of liberation and its aftermath'.[6] In wanting to define a new citizen, these nations cut
people off from the vital source of meaning they had, religion,
which later comes back to haunt the very polity that had tried
to expunge it, with the force of revenge.
    Walzer's account elicits at least two questions: 1) Was
the secular nationalism of recently constituted, non-Christian
nations such as Israel (or India and Algeria for that matter)
indeed as absolutist, secular and universalist as he claims?
2) Was such an 'absolutist' secular culture responsible for
religious revivalism in its denial of people's need for religion?
    As Walzer rightly claims, Zionism was in its inception a
militantly secular movement. It was secular not only because
it wanted to shake its people from the torpor of religiosity
but because it embraced with love and fervour the secularity of the high culture of the nations in which Jews lived,
whether Russia, Germany, France or Great Britain. Jews had
long been a part of the West, far less ambivalently, and far
more intimately than those of the colonized nations Walzer
discusses. In that sense, Jews had not been 'colonized' as
Indians or Algerians had been. On the contrary, throughout

the eighteenth and nineteenth centuries, Jews embraced the West in a symbiotic relationship, a process which the Enlightenment only accentuated since the idea of universality promised to redeem all human beings. When they left Europe for British Mandate Palestine, Zionists viewed themselves as representatives of such a culture. The Zionist project was thus at one and the same time a project to provide national sovereignty to a particular people and a project to export Western European secular culture to the Middle East. In that sense, Zionism was a far more complex national project than the liberation of India or Algeria in that it was at once colonialist *and* emancipatory.

The Janus face of a secular culture and a religious state

Walzer is right when he states that the majority of the Jewish people who fought for the creation of a state were secular, but their secularity was not, or not only, the result of Zionist nationalism: it was the result of a process of modernization that had begun before Jewish nationalism per se. It was the secularization of the Jews that fostered the nationalist project rather than the other way round. Zionism was in fact a great historical compromise between the desire of assimilation to a European vision Zionists revered and the desire to maintain Jewish identity by renewing it in the form of political sovereignty. In light of this, it is not surprising that all or most key national symbols of Israel, the rhetoric of the return to Zion and the public calendar, were directly borrowed from religious symbolism (for example, the two blue stripes in the flag represent a *tallit* or prayer shawl, and the blue and white colours are mentioned in the Bible). In addition, far from negating religious Judaism, Zionism made surprising concessions to it in the institutional organization of the state itself. In 1947, Ben-Gurion wrote a famous letter to Agudat Israel, the organization representing Ashkenazi Orthodox Judaism, committing the state to four key religious aspects of collective life: Shabbat observance; *kashrout* (the observance of Jewish dietary laws) in the army; control of personal laws by rabbis; and the autonomy of the religious education

system.[7] More significantly and dramatically, the Law of
Return granted automatic citizenship to anyone defined as
a Jew (in 1970 it was extended to persons with one Jewish
grandparent), paving the way for an ethnic, descent-based
definition of citizenship. Furthermore, inside the state, only
rabbis were granted the authority to ascertain who was or
was not Jewish, and thus to decide on the identity of those
who could claim the privileges attendant to such Jewishness
(e.g., a non-Jewish woman cannot marry a Jewish man since
orthodox rabbis forbid such marriages; nor can their children be considered Jewish). Religion thus controlled what
is perhaps the single most authoritative prerogative of the
state, namely the capacity to define who can or cannot be
a citizen and what his or her privileges are. Zionism, which
had displayed such extraordinary resourcefulness, displayed
an astonishing lack of imagination when it came to the most
fundamental element of national life.

Perhaps Walzer would not consider all of these concessions an 'engagement with Judaism', viewing them as arduous
political compromises which did not require a deep com-
mitment in the souls of the nationalist revolutionaries. But
he commits the same fallacy as the Israelis of the time: he
confuses high and official culture – deeply secular indeed
– and institution-building, which in due time mattered far
more than high culture and eventually subverted it. If the
early Zionists were proficient in the universalist language of
Weltliteratur and the Marxian language of socialist redistribution, they were far less proficient in the universalist liberal
language of human rights and citizenship, precisely because
they were reluctant to imagine the boundaries of their new
nation in terms other than those that had been drawn up by
religion. The Israeli polity was thus characterized by a gap
between its official culture and its chief political institution –
the state. It was this breach that enabled determined zealots
and fundamentalist groups to seize power.

Thus, while I agree with Walzer that the connection
between nationalism and religion is not a necessary one (see
the French case), in the case of Israel this relation was present
from the beginning (I suspect this is also true in the Alge-
rian case, as Jean Birnbaum shows in his remarkable book
Un silence religieux).[8] Through a combination of political

strategies it shaped and dictated a habitual and unconscious reference and deference to religion and a culture rooted in the Bible, constituting a thick national identity quite different from the thin one of conventional Christian liberalism. It was thick because it created an oblique equivalence between Jewishness and Israeli citizenship, between Jewishness and the state. Such thick national identity places Israel in a political category in itself, between the liberal countries of the West and the religious/ethnicity-based membership of surrounding Muslim nations. Unlike the former and much like the latter, it blurred the institutional distinction between state and religion. As Étienne Balibar put it in *Saeculum*, separating the secular from the religious is crucial in order to *free* the state for the function of spreading a common civic culture.[9] When the state is not free to accomplish this function, it becomes easier for one group to view itself as its sole legitimate representative and to create hierarchies of membership. Inscribed thus in the history of the Israeli nation was a definition of citizenship based on blood descent and religion, which undermined one major historical promise of nationalism, namely its inclusiveness. It was thus a strange state: strong as a Goliath militarily but internally weak, as it willingly gave up its chief prerogative to the religious clergy, making it not only weak but also ridden with internal contradictions.

The big bang of Israeli politics

That Israeli state building was neither secular nor universalist and yet contained elements of Western colonialism is of course apparent when we consider the Arab population, but it is even sharper and clearer in another case, a case which *in fine* constitutes the central, crucial event from which all subsequent Israeli populist politics derived. As in Western countries, it has to do with immigrants and with the way in which they are treated by established elites.

A few years after the Declaration of Independence in 1948, Jews of Middle Eastern and North African origins started flocking to Israel and were immediately excluded from all significant areas of social power. While European Jews, the Ashkenazim, were usually placed in urban centres where wealth was generated, Yemenite, Moroccan and Iraqi Jews were sent to faraway geographical locations euphemistically known as the 'periphery', which considerably slowed down their social, economic and cultural integration (a comparative analysis of the fate of the same Jews in Israel and in other countries such as Canada and France demonstrates their extraordinary exclusion from Israeli society).[10] More crucially perhaps, Jews from Arab countries were classified by the Zionist establishment as a single, unified category – the 'Mizrahim' – in an act of Orientalism par excellence, emanating from a binary logic by which 'Mizrahim' were bestowed a presumably non-European identity radically different from that of the Ashkenazim.[11] The fate of the Mizrahim was curiously similar to that of the workers who were brought to European countries, such as the Maghreban workforce in France, colonial populations in England and Turks in Germany. Like their European counterparts, Ashkenazi Zionists allocated working-class jobs to Mizrahim: men worked as truck drivers, wood cutters, factory workers; women worked as housemaids, or in factories. As a single entity, Jews from Arab countries were classified as inferior to their European counterparts in any and all respects. For the many distinguished professors, psychologists and state officials who expressed themselves on the topic, Mizrahim were of 'inferior intelligence', 'primitive', 'culturally backward', pre-modern and, most of all, religious, therefore doubly foreign to the progressive Western-inspired Zionist secular state.[12] But there is an irony here: the religiosity of Jews coming from Arab countries was far more modern and modernizing than that of their ultra-orthodox Ashkenazi counterparts. What the Zionists took to be the religiosity of Mizrahim was the effect of their Orientalization by the Western-aspiring state of Israel.[13] While Agudat Israel (with which Ben-Gurion had so easily compromised) was by any standard religiously extremist, anti-modern and ultra-orthodox, the religiosity of Jews born in Arab countries was far more accommodating of Western values. Ashkenazi anti-modern, ultra-orthodox, fundamentalist religion had been smoothly woven into the fabric of the state apparatus, but the far more progressive and modern religiosity of Mizrahim was rejected. Worse than that, their religiosity became a mark of cultural and social inferiority, and secularity became a mark of cultural distinction and symbolic domination.

To this we must add the fact that the reigning left parties practised a generalized nepotism by installing 'their own' people in influential economic, academic and political positions. It is thus rather easy to understand why, when the leader of the right-wing revisionist movement Menachem Begin embraced the Mizrahim, they deserted the Labor Party in droves. Mizrahim, seeing themselves as left behind and excluded, did what any rational actor would do: they voted for Menachem Begin's party.

This was the big bang of Israeli politics, the event to which we can trace back the birth of populist politics, the irrevocable demise of the left, and the shift to identitarian, ethnic and racial politics. Begin embraced Mizrahim *as* Jews, and thus offered what the left had not been able to offer: equality with Ashkenazim on the basis of Jewishness.[14] Begin thus enabled a far more direct and straightforward connection between the Jewish state and the hitherto secular political culture of Israel. Mizrahim supported Begin and have never since left the new political orbit he created. In embracing them as Jews, Begin – who was committed to the rule of law and to human rights – was unknowingly paving the way for the strong men of the present, by creating the conditions for what became a majoritarian politics catering to all Israelis *as* Jews.

When Begin became prime minister in 1977, Mizrahim constituted a sizeable portion of the Jewish population, certainly one without which elections could not be won. The fact that until the late 1970s no Ashkenazi political leader had addressed the social or cultural aspirations of Mizrahim (let alone was aware of their stunning exclusion) is evidence of the extraordinary blindness of that leadership, a blindness which had its source in a simple sociological fact: the left was at one and the same time the defender of liberal values and the dominant class in all aspects of social life. As such, it was endowed with an unshakable sense of cultural and economic superiority. It disdainfully exploited Mizrahim, using them as a workforce to settle the land and build up industries. In Israel, many of the Mizrahim suffered a severe loss of status in comparison to the one they had had in their native Arab countries (that is certainly true for Moroccan Jews), and their fate bears a family resemblance to the ways in which Western colonialists treated the natives in Africa, India or the Middle East and later the immigrant workers who came to rebuild post-Second World War Western Europe. Little wonder then that Mizrahim – who are now 50 per cent of the population – developed a deep distrust of anything left, secular and liberal, especially the pious Ashkenazi rhetoric of universalism, which the Mizrahim viewed as nothing but an empty shell covering up the astounding economic, political and cultural privileges the Ashkenazim had amassed.

The extraordinary blindness of the Labor leadership to the role that the exclusion of Mizrahim has played in destroying the left and in radicalizing the right continues to this day: the Labor party has very few Mizrahi representatives – except as 'token Mizrahim'; it has never really addressed or apologized for its historical mistreatment of Mizrahim (an exception was Ehud Barak's 1997 apology when he was the leader of the Labor party); most Ashkenazi academics, politicians and intellectuals ignore the issue entirely and regularly dismiss it as a manifestation of 'Mizrahi whiny ungratefulness'.[15] Few 'enlightened' groups in the world have been as successful as the Israeli Ashkenazim at denying and erasing their history of ethnic domination.

This is why, despite the fact that Likud did little to lift people from the 'periphery', the Mizrahi's allegiance to the right remained unchallenged, since their exclusion by the secular left was still deeply inscribed in their collective memory. Even while Netanyahu has liberalized the economy (moving Israeli factories abroad, taking away working-class jobs the socialist party had secured and thus widening inequalities), and consistently served the rich and the powerful throughout his many years in power, the Mizrahim have remained in the orbit of the right.

After Begin's victory in 1977, the Jewish empowerment of Mizrahim through their Jewishness percolated into Israeli society. In 1984 Mizrahim created the fundamentalist Shas party, which has been a significant player in Israeli politics ever since. As Amnon Raz-Krakotzkin states, Mizrahim could enter politics only as an ultra-orthodox religious party because the state viewed Jews and Arabs as two radically distinct entities and because it had denied Mizrahim the possibility of a secular identity.[16] It should thus be clear that the fundamentalism of the Mizrahim did not precede their arrival in Israel, but was, and ironically so, a creation of their interaction with the Western and secular society the Ashkenazim had built.[17] It was not in any way a recovery of a lost authentic identity.

Shas became the only political party prepared to organize the working classes. Through a large network of charitable organizations it provided meals to hungry children, help to poor families and religious education – in short, it stepped in where the state and the left were not to be found.[18] This is why Shas was able to transform the values of Mizrahim: many of them had arrived from modern cities, and were engaged in a process of secularization, but through Shas and the Likud they withdrew into a regressive fundamentalist politics. In the coalition system of Israeli politics, Shas had power. It frequently took two portfolios: the ministry of the interior and the ministry of religious services.

In line with the new importance of Jewishness in Israeli politics, one of the effects of the Shas influence over these portfolios in the 1980s and 1990s was to severely limit the immigration of workers in the care industry from countries such as Romania and the Philippines, so as not to threaten the 'Jewish character' of the country.[19] In the 1990s Israel thus started practising the kind of immigration policy today advocated by the US white-supremacist alt-right that has crowned Donald Trump. To quote one of its prominent representatives, Richard Spencer, famous for saluting Trump with a raised arm and a 'Hail Trump': 'if Sheldon Adelson would promote the same immigration policy in the United States that Israel has, I would think that is a good thing'.[20] The admiration seems mutual. None other than Shas' leader Aryeh Deri has claimed that Trump's election signals the imminent arrival of the Messiah: 'If such a miracle like this can happen we have already reached the days of the Messiah, therefore we are really in the era of the birth pangs of the Messiah.'[21]

The effect of three decades of Shas's presence in Israeli politics has been to create a slow habituation to a politics of ethnic and religious purity which excludes non-Jews from the body politic, gives exclusive power to orthodox over other Jewish denominations, and aims to control the purity of

the Jewish race by passing more stringent laws on marriage
with non-Jews.

A tragic end

So this story has a tragic end. The association between Ashkenazi secularism, economic exclusion and cultural arrogance
became so entrenched that it was virtually impossible to turn
secular, socialist, liberal ideas into credible political options
for the downtrodden.[22] Hence, the weakness of the Israeli
left is due to the simple fact it never represented the working
classes. But mostly this is about the tragedy of a group who
had the unique opportunity to bridge the gap between Arabs
and Jews, between modernity and tradition, between Europe
and the Middle East, Judaism and Islam, and failed at it
because fundamentalism was its way of entering politics. The
secular Ashkenazi left wasted this opportunity – and so we
ended up with a Jewish version of ethnic, racial and religious
supremacy.

Should we then see Israel as the vanguard of the global shift
towards populism? The analogies between (a large section of)
Mizrahim voting for Likud and Shas and Trumpists are striking: like Trump voters, lots of Mizrahim live outside urban
centres; like them, they have seen urban elites amass riches
and defend the rights of sexual and cultural minorities; they
also live in a country where manufacturing jobs have been
jeopardized by neoliberal policies; they have far less access
to higher education than left-wing Ashkenazim; and finally,
like Trump voters, they harbour a deep resentment against
elites who in fact never represented them. (This, incidentally,
is why Mizrahi Jews have been in favour of the privatization
of higher education. While Mizrahim were and continue to
be vastly under-represented in state-sponsored universities,
private colleges have embraced them.[23])

Shas fundamentalists are not the only racists in town. They
are obviously complemented by the zealots, the messianic
settlers. Nor are they directly responsible for the attempts to
curtail freedom of speech and the weakening of the status of
Arab minorities. But they are definitely responsible for inau-
gurating a politics of Jewishness, legitimizing and spreading

the idea that liberal ideas are anti-Jewish, that secular law should be replaced by religious law, and that Israel should be cleansed of non-Jewish immigrants. Miri Regev, the current minister of culture and sport, offers a striking example of a Likud politician who uses her proud Mizrahi identity and the former exclusion of Mizrahim to justify cultural 'purges' and initiatives to crush the power of liberal secular elites in culture.

This reading of the relationship of the Israeli state to religion thus suggests a double particularity: Israel created a state whose citizenship was simultaneously ethnic and religious but it also created an internal neo-colonialism in the form of the Orientalization of the Mizrahi Jews. Both had the same source: a state which did not view itself as entrusted with the mission of creating a common civic national democratic culture blind to ethnic and religious differences. Far from having suffered from an excess of universalism and secularity which failed to engage with religion, as Walzer claims, it is rather the other way round: it is precisely the fact that Israel was neither universalist nor secular that paved a political and cultural highway for fundamentalist movements to claim to be the true representatives of a state which conceived of itself as the state of Jews.

In this context, it made perfect sense for Mizrahim to take recourse to Jewish supremacy as a political strategy. While with Trumpists the economic elites responsible for the disappearance of working-class jobs were by and large distinct from the cultural elites promoting all-inclusiveness for immigrants and LGBTQ, in Israel these elites were one and the same. The people who excluded the Mizrahim were exactly those groups that professed equality while retaining tight control over cultural, political and economic institutions. Fundamentalist Mizrahim and Trump alt-rightists are insurgent, anti-establishment and deeply regressive political movements only inasmuch as they were not adequately represented by the liberal left and inasmuch as the left has been associated with privilege. While universalism was the main strategy for working classes and minorities to gain equality during the nineteenth and twentieth centuries, national and religious particularism has now become the preferred strategy of the excluded. This crisis is thus about the liberal elites, who constructed a world in which universalism, globalization and cosmopolitanism could be converted into currencies as symbolic and economic capital, and about the fact that those elites defended minorities in ways that came increasingly to jar with the struggles of ordinary working-class people.

In Israel, the academic left massively ignored or denied altogether the plight of Mizrahim and fought mostly for women and gays (less prominently for the Arab minority). That someone of the stature of Michael Walzer simply pays no attention to a social group as large as the Mizrahim in a book supposed to be analysing the retreat to fundamentalism in Israel is a depressing illustration of the ways in which Jewish liberal-left historiography and sociology suffer from the same blindness that underpinned social domination. Squarely at the centre of Israeli history and yet largely unacknowledged is a gigantic class and ethnic conflict that has driven the whole of Israeli politics.

The task of the left

Right-wing populism thrives because the world of the working classes has been destroyed by corporate capitalism and has become devalued by cultural progressive elites who, from the 1980s onwards, focused their intellectual and political energy on sexual and cultural minorities, thus generating fierce culture wars. Once the world of the working classes was destroyed and spurned, it could be restored through promises of lost racial, religious and ethnic privileges.

Trump's election is a wake-up call for the left throughout the world. However polarized the worlds of the cultural elites and the conservative working-class may have become, the left has no choice but to re-engage with the moral world of lives that have been torn asunder by the rippling effects of colonialism and capitalism. Short of that, in the long run liberalism may be doomed to extinction.

Notes

1 Christophe Ayad, 'L'israélisation du monde (occidental)', *Le Monde*, 1 December 2016.

2 Allison Kaplan Sommer, 'Jews-only Poll Highlights Israeli Youths' Drift to the Right', *Haaretz*, 13 April 2016.

3 Michael Walzer, *The Paradox of Liberation: Secular Revolutions and Religious Counterrevolutions*, New Haven: Yale University Press, 2015, p. xii.

4 Ibid., p. 7.

5 Ibid., p. 22.

6 Ibid., p. 24.

7 Itamar Rabinovich and Jehuda Reinharz, *Israel in the Middle East: Documents and Readings on Society, Politics, and Foreign Relations Pre-1948 to the Present*, Waltham, MA: Brandeis University Press, 2008, pp. 58–9.

8 Jean Birnbaum, *Un silence religieux. La gauche face djihadisme*, Paris: Seuil, 2016.

9 Étienne Balibar, *Saeculum. Culture, religion, idéologie*, Paris: Galilée, 2012.

10 Baruch Kimmerling, *'Inequality and Discrimination': The End of Ashkenazi Hegemony*, Jerusalem: Keter, 2001 (in Hebrew), pp. 21–9.

11 Aziza Khazzoom, 'The Great Chain of Orientalism: Jewish Identity, Stigma Management, and Ethnic Exclusion in Israel', *American Sociological Review*, 68:4 (2003), pp. 481–510; Amnon Raz-Krakotzkin, 'The Zionist Return to the West and the Mizrahi Jewish Perspective', in Ivan Davidson Kalmar and Derek J. Penslar (eds), *Orientalism and the Jews*, Waltham, MA: Brandeis University Press, 2005, pp. 162–81; Ella Shohat, 'The Invention of the Mizrahim', *Journal of Palestine Studies*, 29:1 (1999), pp. 5–20.

12 Sami Shalom Chetrit, *Intra-Jewish Conflict in Israel: White Jews, Black Jews*, London and New York: Routledge, 2009; Sammy Smooha, 'The Mass Immigrations to Israel: A Comparison of the Failure of the Mizrahi Immigrants of the 1950s with the Success of the Russian Immigrants of the 1990s', *Journal of Israeli History*, 27:1 (2008), pp. 1–27.

13 Yehouda A. Shenhav, *The Arab Jews: A Postcolonial Reading of Nationalism, Religion, and Ethnicity*, Stanford: Stanford University Press, 2006.

14 For the same line of argument explaining the success of Shas see Yoav Peled, 'Towards a Redefinition of Jewish Nationalism in Israel? The Enigma of Shas', *Ethnic and Racial Studies*, 21:4 (1998), pp. 703–27.

15 When the Moroccan-born Amir Peretz became the leader of the Labor Party in 2005, Shimon Peres left the party in outrage and joined the centre-right party Kadima. Peres was not alone: many

traditional Labor voters voted for Kadima in the 2006 election, so unrecognizable for them was a Labor party led by a Mizrahi.

16 Amnon Raz-Krakotzkin, 'A National Colonial Theology: Religion, Orientalism, and the Construction of the Secular in Zionist Discourse', *Tel Aviver Jahrbuch für Deutsche Geschichte*, 31 (2002), pp. 312–26; Raz-Krakotzkin, 'The Zionist Return to the West and the Mizrahi Jewish Perspective'.

17 Shlomo Deshen, 'The Emergence of the Israeli Sephardi Ultra-orthodox Movement', *Jewish Social Studies*, 11:2 (2005), pp. 77–101.

18 Eitan Schiffman, 'The Shas School System in Israel', *Nationalism and Ethnic Politics*, 11:1 (2005), pp. 89–124.

19 Ami Pedahzur, 'The Transformation of Israel's Extreme Right', *Studies in Conflict and Terrorism*, 24:1 (2001), pp. 25–42.

20 Taly Krupkin, 'Alt-right Leader Has No Regrets About "Hail Trump", But Tells Haaretz: Jews Have Nothing to Fear', *Haaretz*, 3 December 2016.

21 Jeremy Sharon, '"Trump's Election Heralds Coming of Messiah", Says Deri', *Jerusalem Post*, 10 November 2016.

22 For a brilliant analysis of the failure of universalist messages in Israel see Nissim Mizrachi, 'Sociology in the Garden: Beyond the Liberal Grammar of Contemporary Sociology', *Israel Studies Review*, 31:1 (2016), pp. 36–65.

23 For the relevant data see Hanna Ayalon, 'Social Implications of the Expansion and Diversification of Higher Education in Israel', *Israeli Sociology*, 10 (2008), pp. 33–60 (in Hebrew).

6

Majoritarian futures

Ivan Krastev

In his novel *Death with Interruptions* (2008), José Saramago tells the story of a country where people suddenly stop dying and death loses its central role in human life. At first, people are gripped by euphoria, but soon 'awkwardness' of various kinds – metaphysical, political and practical – starts to come back into their world. The Catholic Church realizes that 'without death there is no resurrection, and without resurrection there is no church'.[1] For insurance companies, life without death also means oblivion. The state faces the impossible task of paying pensions forever. Families with elderly and infirm relatives become aware that it is only death that saves them from an eternity of nursing care. A mafia-style cabal emerges to smuggle old and sick people to neighbouring countries (where death is still an option). The prime minister warns the monarch: 'If we don't start dying again, we have no future.'[2]

Saramago is short on details regarding the political turmoil in the unnamed 'End-of-Death-Land', but we can easily imagine 'occupy movements' in which young and unemployed people stage protests and occupy public squares once they discover there will be no jobs for them in this 'land of no death', and that the politics of the place will be dominated by older generations. It is also easy to assume the rise of 'great again' right-wing populist parties and leaders. In short, Saramago's novel is a great introduction to today's world.

The West's experience with globalization resembles Saramago's imagined flirtation with immortality. It is a dream that suddenly turned into a nightmare. Just a few years ago, many in the West tended to view the opening up of the world as the end of all troubles. This enthusiasm has vanished. Instead, we are witnessing a worldwide insurgence against the progressive post-1989 liberal order defined by the opening of borders for people, capital, goods and ideas, an insurgence that takes the form of democracy's revolt against liberalism.

The paradoxical effect of the spread of democracy in the non-Western world, according to a recent study, is that citizens

> in a number of supposedly consolidated democracies in North America and Western Europe have not only grown more critical of their political leaders. Rather, they have also become more cynical about the value of democracy as a political system, less hopeful that anything they do might influence public policy, and more willing to express support for authoritarian alternatives.[3]

The study also shows that 'younger generations are less committed to the importance of democracy' and that they are 'less likely to be politically engaged'.[4]

No less puzzling are the effects of the revolution in communications. Today people can Google virtually everything there is to know about the world, and censorship has become practically impossible. At the same time, we can observe a stunning spread of abstruse conspiracy theories and a dramatic rise in public mistrust of democratic institutions. The irony is that the death of censorship has brought us post-truth politics.

What we witness in the West today is not a temporary setback in a progressive development, not a 'pause', but a reversal. It is the unmaking of the post-1989 world, and the most dramatic feature of this ongoing transformation is not the rise of authoritarian regimes, but the changing nature of democratic ones in many Western countries. In the first decades after 1989 the spread of free elections meant the inclusion of different minority groups (ethnic, religious, sexual) in public life. Today elections foster the empowerment of majority groups. Threatened majorities have emerged as the major force in European politics. They fear that foreigners are taking over their countries and endangering their way of life, and they are convinced that this is the result of a conspiracy between cosmopolitan-minded elites and tribal-minded immigrants. The populism of these majorities is not the product of romantic nationalism, as might have been the case a century or more ago. Rather, it is fuelled by demographic projections that foreshadow not only the expected mass movements of people to Europe and the US but also the shrinking role of both globally, as well as by the disruptions brought about by the technological revolution. Demography makes Europeans imagine a world in which their cultures are vanishing, while the technological revolution promises them a world in which their current jobs will disappear. The transformation of Western public opinion from a revolutionary into a reactionary force explains the rise of right-wing populist parties in Europe and the victory of Donald Trump in the US.

The end of...?

A little more than a quarter-century ago, in what now seems like the very distant year of 1989 – the *annus mirabilis* that saw Germans dancing joyfully on the rubble of the Berlin Wall – Francis Fukuyama captured the spirit of the time. With the end of the Cold War, he argued in a famous essay, all major ideological conflicts had been resolved.[5] The contest was over, and history had produced a winner: Western-style liberal democracy. Taking a page from Hegel, Fukuyama presented the victory of the West in the Cold War as a favourable verdict delivered by History itself, understood as a kind of Higher Court of World Justice. In the short run, some countries might not succeed in emulating this exemplary model. But they would have to try. The Western model was the only (i)deal in town.

Within this framework, the central questions were: how can the West transform the rest of the world and how can the rest of the world best imitate the West? What institutions and

policies need to be transferred and copied? It is this vision of
the post-Cold War world that is collapsing before our eyes.
The question posed by the unravelling of the liberal order is
how the last three decades have transformed the West and
why the post-1989 world is resented by those who, in the
eyes of many, were its principal beneficiaries: Americans and
Europeans. The current political turmoil in Europe and the
US cannot be reduced to a revolt of the economic losers from
globalization. The strongest argument supporting the view
that it is not only about the economy cites the case of Poland:
Poles enjoyed a decade of impressive economic growth, prosperity and even the decline of social inequality; nevertheless
in 2015 they voted for a reactionary populist party that they
had voted out of power just a few years earlier. Why did
they do that?

   At the same time as Fukuyama was heralding history's end,
the American political scientist Ken Jowitt was presenting a
very different interpretation of the end of the Cold War – not
as a time of triumph but as the onset of crisis and trauma, a
time when the seeds were sown for what he called 'the new
world disorder'.[6] In his view, the end of communism 'should
be likened to a catastrophic volcanic eruption, one that initially and immediately affects only the surrounding political
"biota" (i.e., other Leninist regimes), but whose effects most
likely will have a global impact on the boundaries and identities that for half a century have politically, economically, and
militarily defined and ordered the world'.[7] In Fukuyama's
view, the borders between states would formally endure
in the post-Cold War, but they would lose much of their
relevance. Jowitt, on the other hand, envisioned redrawn
borders, reshaped identities, proliferating conflicts and para-
lyzing uncertainty. He saw the post-communist period not as
an age of imitation with few dramatic events, but as a painful
and dangerous era full of regimes that could best be described
as political mutants.

   Jowitt agreed with Fukuyama that no new universal ideology would appear to challenge liberal democracy, but he
foresaw the return of old ethnic, religious and tribal identities. And indeed, one of the paradoxes of globalization is that
while the free movement of people, capital, goods and ideas
brings people closer to each other, it also reduces the capacity

of nation-states to integrate strangers. As Arjun Appadurai observed a decade ago, 'the nation state has been steadily reduced to the fiction of its ethnos as the last cultural resource over which it may exercise full domination'.[8] The unintended consequence of macroeconomic policies following the mantra 'there is no alternative' is that identity politics have taken over the centre of European politics. The market and the internet have proven to be powerful forces for increasing the choices of individuals, but they have eroded the social cohesion of Western societies because both reinforce the inclination of individuals to satisfy their natural preferences, such as preferring contact with people like themselves and staying away from strangers. We live in a world that is more connected but also less integrated. Globalization connects while disconnecting. Jowitt warned that in this connected/disconnected world we should be prepared for explosions of anger and the emergence of 'movements of rage' that would spring from the ashes of weakened nation-states.

For Jowitt the post-Cold War order was more like 'a singles bar of a kind': 'It's a bunch of people who don't know each other, who, in the lingo, hook up, go home, have sex, don't see each other again, can't remember each other's names, go back to the bar and meet somebody else. So it's a world that's made up of disconnections.'[9] This is a world rich in experience, but it does not lend itself to stable identities and it does not engender loyalties. Not surprisingly, as a reaction, we see the return of the barricade as the desired border.

It is exactly this transition – from the disconnected world of the 1990s to the barricaded world emerging today – that has changed the role performed by democratic regimes. It replaces democracy as a regime favouring the emancipation of minorities with democracy as a political regime that secures the power of majorities.

The current refugee crisis in Europe is the most striking manifestation of the changing nature of the appeal of democracy and the rising tension between the principles of democratic majoritarianism and liberal constitutionalism for both the publics and the elites. The Hungarian prime minister Viktor Orbán spoke for many when he claimed that 'a democracy is not necessarily liberal. Just because something is not liberal, it still can be a democracy.'[10] Moreover, he insisted, one could – and indeed should – say that societies founded upon liberal principles will likely not be able to sustain their global competitiveness in coming years. Rather, it is more likely they will suffer a setback, unless they manage to reform themselves substantially:

> Today, the stars of international analyses are Singapore, China, India, Turkey, Russia. And I believe that our political community rightly anticipated this challenge. And if we think on what we did in the last four years, and what we are going to do in the following four years, then it really can be interpreted from this angle. We are searching for (and we are doing our best to find ways of parting with Western European dogmas, making ourselves independent from them) the form of organizing a community, that is capable of making us competitive in this great world-race.[11]

The migration crisis, whatever EU officials in Brussels might say, is not about a 'lack of solidarity'. Rather, it is about a clash of solidarities – of national, ethnic and religious solidarities chafing against our obligations as human beings. It should be seen not simply as the movement of people from outside Europe to the old continent, or from poorer EU member states to richer ones, but also in terms of the movement of voters away from the centre, and of the displacement of the division between left and right by the division between internationalists and nativists.

The refugee crisis also sparked a migration of arguments. In the 1970s left-wing intellectuals in the West tended to defend passionately the right of poor indigenous communities in India or Latin America to preserve their way of life. But what about the middle-class communities in the West today? Are they to be deprived of the very same right? And how should we explain the fact that it is the traditional constituency of the left that is moving to the far right? In Austria, more than 85 per cent of blue-collar workers voted for the extreme national-conservative candidate in the second round of the May 2016 presidential elections. In German regional elections in the northern state of Mecklenburg-Vorpommern, more than 30 per cent of the same group supported Alternative für Deutschland. In the French regional elections in December 2015, the National Front won 50 per cent of the vote among working-class voters. The results of the British referendum are equally striking: Brexit polled strongest in the traditional 'safe' Labour constituencies in the north of England. It is now clear that the post-Marxist working class, which today believes neither in its vanguard role nor in a global anti-capitalist revolution, has no reason to be internationalist.

Normative threats

The populism of the threatened majorities is a kind of populism for which history has poorly prepared us. It is psychologists rather than sociologists who can help us make sense of it. In the 1930s and 1940s some German émigrés who were lucky enough to escape the country before the Nazis could send them to concentration camps were haunted by the question of whether what they saw happening in Germany could happen in their new homelands. They were not content to explain authoritarianism simply in terms of the German national character or in terms of class politics. They were disposed to look at authoritarianism as a stable characteristic of an individual, as a certain type of personality. Since the 1950s the study of the 'authoritarian personality' has undergone major changes and the original hypothesis has been significantly reformulated, but in her recent book *The Authoritarian Dynamic* Karen Stenner,[12] who works in this tradition, presents several findings that are of particular relevance for our attempt to understand the rise of threatened majorities and the changing nature of Western democracies. Stenner demonstrates that the demand for authoritarian rule is not a stable psychological trait. It is rather a psychological predisposition of individuals to become intolerant when they perceive increased levels of threat.

In Jonathan Haidt's words, it's 'as though some people have a button on their foreheads, and when the button is pushed, they suddenly become intensely focused on defending their in-group, kicking out foreigners and non-conformists, and stamping out dissent within the group'.[13] And what pushes this button is not just any threat, but what Stenner calls a 'normative threat', when the person has the feeling

that the integrity of the moral order is endangered and the
perceived 'we' is falling apart. It is a fear that the moral order
is collapsing, rather than his concrete situation, that triggers
his turn against foreigners and any others whom he sees as
a threat.

Stenner's notion of the 'normative threat' helps us to
understand better how the refugee crisis of 2015 has transformed European politics and why Central European societies were the ones that expressed the most hostile reactions,
despite the fact that there are hardly any refugees in their
countries. In the case of Europe, the 'normative threat' posed
by the refugee crisis has its roots in demographics. Curiously, demographic panic is one of the least discussed factors
shaping Europeans' behaviour towards migrants and refugees. But it is a critical one, and particularly important in
Central and Eastern Europe. In the region's recent history,
nations and states have been known to wither. Over the
last quarter-century, about one in ten Bulgarians has left to
live and work abroad. And the majority of those who left
(and leave) are, as one would expect, young people. According to UN projections, Bulgaria's population will shrink
by 27.9 per cent between now and 2050. In small nations
like Bulgaria, Lithuania or Romania (over the last ten years
Lithuania has lost 12.2 per cent of its population, Romania
7 per cent), alarm over 'ethnic disappearance' can be felt.
For them, the arrival of migrants signals their exit from
history, and the popular argument that an ageing Europe
needs migrants only strengthens a growing sense of existential
melancholy.

A decade ago, the Hungarian philosopher and former dissident Gáspár Miklós Tamás[14] observed that the Enlightenment, in which the idea of the European Union is intellectually
rooted, demands universal citizenship. But universal citizenship requires one of two things to happen: either poor and
dysfunctional countries have to become places in which it
is worthwhile to live, or Europe has to open its borders
to everybody. Neither is going to happen anytime soon, if
ever. Today the world is populated by many failed states
nobody wants to be a citizen of, and Europe does not have
the capacity, nor will its citizens ever agree, to keep the
borders open.

The migrants' revolution

In 1981, when researchers of the University of Michigan conducted the first World Values Survey,[15] they were surprised to find that a nation's happiness was not determined by its material well-being. Back then Nigerians were as happy as West Germans. But now, thirty-five years later, the situation has changed. According to the latest surveys, in most places people are as happy as their GDP would suggest.[16] What happened in between was that Nigerians got TV sets and later the internet, which made it possible for young Africans to see how Europeans live and what their schools and hospitals look like. Globalization has made the world a village, but this village lives under a dictatorship – the dictatorship of global comparisons. People do not compare their lives with those of their neighbours any more. They compare themselves with the most prosperous inhabitants of the planet.

In this connected world of ours, migration is the new revolution – not the twentieth-century revolution of the masses, but a twenty-first-century exit-driven revolution enacted by individuals and families and inspired not by pictures of the future painted by ideologues but by Google Maps' photos of life on the other side of the border. This new revolution does not require political movements or political leaders to succeed. So we should not be surprised if, for many of the wretched of the earth, crossing the EU's border is more attractive than any utopia. For a growing number of people, the idea of change means changing the country they live in rather than the government they live under.

The problem with this migrants' revolution is its worrying capacity to provoke a counter-revolution in Europe. The key characteristic of many of the right-wing populist parties in Europe is not that they are national-conservative but that they are reactionary. Reflecting on the rise of reactionary politics in the West, Mark Lilla has observed that 'the enduring vitality of the reactionary spirit even in the absence of a revolutionary political program' comes from the feeling that to 'live a modern life anywhere in the world today, subject to perpetual social and technological changes, is to experience the psychological equivalent of permanent revolution'.[17] And for the reactionaries, 'the only sane response to apocalypse is to provoke another, in hopes of starting over'.[18]

The Harvard economist Dani Rodrik turned out to be right with his warning some years ago that in order to manage the tensions between national democracy and the global market, nations have three options. They can restrict democracy in order to gain competitiveness in international markets. They can limit globalization in the hope of building democratic legitimacy at home. Or they can globalize democracy at the cost of national sovereignty. What we cannot have is hyper-globalization, democracy and self-determination all at once. So it should come as no surprise when internationalists begin to feel uneasy about national democracies and when democracy-praising populists turn out to be protectionist and isolationist.[19]

The populist turn

If history teaches us anything, it is that the spread of free elections can be an instrument for both opening and closing national societies. Democracy is a mechanism of inclusion but also of exclusion, and what we are witnessing today is the rise of majoritarian regimes in which the majority has turned the state into its own private possession – as an answer to the competitive pressure of a world in which popular will is the only source of political legitimacy and global markets are the only source of economic growth.

The 'populist turn' is different in different countries, but we can identify some general similarities. The rise of populist sentiments means a return to political polarization and a more confrontational style of politics (which is not necessarily a negative development). It reverses the process of fragmentation of the political space characterized by the mushrooming of small one-issue political parties and movements, and it makes publics focus not on their individual but on their collective fears. The rise of populism entails a return to a more personalized politics in which political leaders play a very significant role and institutions are most often mistrusted. The left/right divide is replaced by a conflict between internationalists and nativists. The explosion of fears also marks the dissolution of the union between democracy and liberalism that was the distinctive characteristic of the post-1989 world.

The real appeal of liberal democracy is that those defeated in elections need not fear losing too much: electoral defeat means having to regroup and plan for the next contest, not having to flee into exile or go underground while all one's possessions are seized. The little-remarked downside of this is that for the winners, liberal democracy offers no chance of a full and final victory. In pre-democratic times – meaning the bulk of human history – disputes were not settled by peaceful debates and orderly handovers of power. Instead, force ruled: the victorious invaders or the winning parties in a civil war had their vanquished foes at their mercy, free to do with them as they liked. Under liberal democracy, the 'conqueror' gets no such satisfaction. The paradox of liberal democracy is that citizens are freer, but they feel powerless.

The appeal of populist parties is that they promise non-ambiguous victory. They appeal to those who view the separation of powers, so beloved by liberals, not as a way to keep those in power accountable but as an alibi for the elites to evade their electoral promises. Thus, what characterizes populists in power are their constant attempts to dismantle the system of checks and balances and to bring independent institutions like courts, central banks, media outlets and civil society organizations under their control. But populist parties are not only merciless victors – they are also nasty losers. Their conviction that they speak for the majority makes it difficult for them to accept electoral defeat. The result is a growing number of contested elections and the rise of the mentality that 'elections are only fair if we win them'.

In the post-1989 world there was the common presumption that the spread of democracy in the long term would also mean the spread of liberalism. It is this very assumption that is now being questioned by the rise of majoritarian regimes in different corners of the globe. The paradox of the post-Cold War liberal democracies in Europe was that the advancement of personal freedoms and human rights was accompanied by the decline of the power of citizens to change not only governments but also policies with their vote. Now the primacy of politics is back and governments are regaining their capacity to rule but – as it seems today – at the cost of individual freedoms.

Notes

1 José Saramago, *Death with Interruptions*, London: Vintage Books, 2008, p. 8.
2 Ibid., p. 78.
3 Roberto Stefan Foa and Yascha Mounk, 'The Democratic Disconnect', *Journal of Democracy*, 27:3 (2016), pp. 5–17, p. 7.
4 Ibid., p. 10.
5 Francis Fukuyama, 'The End of History?', *National Interest* (summer 1989), pp. 3–18.
6 Ken Jowitt, 'After Leninism: The New World Disorder', *Journal of Democracy*, 2 (winter 1991), pp. 11–20. Jowitt later elaborated his ideas in *The New World Disorder: The Leninist Extinction*, Berkeley: University of California Press, 1992, esp. chapters 7–9.
7 Ibid., p. 259.
8 Arjun Appadurai, *Fear of Small Numbers: An Essay on the Geography of Anger*, Durham, NC: Duke University Press, 2006, p. 23.
9 Harry Kreisler, 'The Individual, Charisma and the Leninist Extinction: A Conversation with Ken Jowitt', 7 December 1999, 'Conversations with History', Series of the Institute of International Studies, UC Berkeley, at http://globetrotter.berkeley.edu/people/Jowitt/jowitt-con0.html (retrieved November 2016), p. 5.
10 Viktor Orbán, Speech at Băile Tuşnad, 26 July 2014; an English translation of the speech is available at http://budapestbeacon.com/public-policy/full-text-of-viktor-orbans-speech-at-baile-tusnad-tusnadfurdo-of-26-july-2014/10592 (retrieved November 2016).
11 Ibid.
12 Karen Stenner, *The Authoritarian Dynamic*, Cambridge and New York: Cambridge University Press, 2010.
13 Jonathan Haidt, 'When and Why Nationalism Beats Globalism', *The American Interest*, 12:1, 10 July 2016.
14 Gáspár Miklós Tamás, 'What is Post-fascism?', 13 September 2001, at https://www.opendemocracy.net/people-newright/article_306.jsp (retrieved November 2016).

15 'History of the World Values Survey Association', at http://www.worldvaluessurvey.org/WVSContents.jsp?CMSID=History (retrieved November 2016).
16 Max Roser, 'Happiness and Life Satisfaction' (2016), at https://ourworldindata.org/happiness-and-life-satisfaction (retrieved November 2016).
17 Mark Lilla, *The Shipwrecked Mind: On Political Reaction*, New York: New York Review Books, 2016, p. xiv.
18 Mark Lilla, 'Republicans for Revolution', *New York Review of Books*, 12 January 2012.
19 Dani Rodrik, *The Globalization Paradox: Democracy and the Future of the World Economy*, New York: W. W. Norton & Company, 2011.

7

Europe as refuge

Bruno Latour

Ever since the American elections of November 2016, at least, things have become clearer.

England has drifted back into its dream of empire, nineteenth-century style; America is seeking to become great again, post-war style, with sepia photos, as in 1950. Europe – continental Europe – now finds itself alone, weak and more divided than ever. Poland is dreaming of an imaginary country; Hungary now wants only 'pure-blooded' Hungarians to live in it; the Dutch, French and Italians are struggling with parties that seek to shut themselves away behind equally imaginary borders. Scotland, Catalonia and Flanders wish to become states. Meanwhile, the Russian Bear is licking its chops and China is finally fulfilling its dream of becoming the 'Middle Kingdom' yet again, while ignoring the interests of its fringe populations.

Europe is being dismembered: it counts less than a hazelnut in a nutcracker. And this time around, it can no longer rely on the United States, now controlled by a new Lord of Misrule.

So maybe this is the right time to reconstruct a United Europe. Oh, not the same one as the founding fathers dreamed up just after the war, based on iron, coal and steel, or more recently on the deluded hope it might escape from history via common rules of standardization or the single currency. No:

if Europe must reunite, this is because of threats just as grave
as those of the 1950s – though the continent now needs to
take its place in a history utterly different from that of the
twentieth century.

Europe faces three threats: the decline of the countries
that invented globalization; climate change; and the need to
provide refuge for millions of migrants and refugees. These
three threats, in fact, are merely different aspects of one single
metamorphosis: the European territory has changed nature,
and we Europeans are all migrating towards lands that need
to be rediscovered and reoccupied.

The first historic event is Brexit. The country that invented
unrestricted markets on land and at sea, the country that
was forever pushing for the European Union to become
nothing more than a vast shop, is the very same country that,
when faced with the sudden arrival in Calais of thousands
of refugees, impulsively decided to stop playing the game
of globalization. It is withdrawing from Europe, and thus
from history, absorbed in dreams of an empire that nobody
believes in any more.

The second historic event: the election of Trump. The
country that imposed its own particular globalization on
the world, and with such violence; the country that built
itself on the basis of migration, while eliminating its earliest
inhabitants; that same country is now entrusting its destiny
to a man who is promising to lock himself away in a fortress,
refusing entry to any refugees, no longer coming to the aid of
any cause that is not rooted in his own soil, while preparing
to intervene anywhere and everywhere in the same casual,
blundering way.

Every man for himself! Full steam backwards! The problem:
there's no longer a home, not for anyone. Shove off! Everyone's going to have to move. Why? Because there's no longer
a planet able to fulfil the dreams of globalization.

This is the third and by far the most important historic
event: *12 December 2015*, in Paris, when the United Nations
Climate Change Conference (COP21) finally reached an
agreement.

The significant thing is not what the delegates decided on;
it is not even that this agreement will be applied (the climate-
change deniers in the White House and the Senate will do all

they can to hamstring it). No, the significant thing is that, on that day, all the countries that signed, to general applause, realized that, if they were all to go ahead and follow their respective modernization plans, there was no planet compatible with their hopes for development. Until then, they had been building castles in the air.

If there is no planet, no earth, no soil, no territory to house the Globe of globalization to which all countries claimed to be heading, what should we do? Either we deny the existence of the problem, or else *we seek to come down to earth*. For each of us, the question now becomes: 'Are you going to keep nursing dreams of escape, or are you going to search for a land in which you and your children might live?' This is what now divides people, much more than knowing whether you are politically on the right or the left.

The United States had two solutions. By finally realizing the extent of the change in circumstances, and the hugeness of their responsibility, they could finally become realistic, leading the free world out of the abyss; or they could sink into denial. Trump seems to have decided to leave America to dream on for a few more years, delaying the possibility of coming down to earth and, instead, dragging other countries down into the abyss.

We Europeans cannot allow ourselves to do this. At the very same time as we are becoming aware of many different threats, we will need to take into our continent millions of people – people who, thanks to the joint impact of war, the failure of globalization, and climate change, will (like us, against us, or with us) be thrown into the search for a land that they and their children can live in. We are going to have to live together with people who have not hitherto shared our traditions, our way of life or our ideals, and who are close to us and foreign to us – terribly close and terribly foreign.

With these migrating peoples, the only thing we have in common is that *we are all deprived of land*. We, the *old Europeans*, are deprived because there is no planet for globalization and we are going to change the entire way we live; they, the *future Europeans*, are deprived because they have had to leave their old, devastated lands, and will need to learn to change the entire way *they* live. Not much to ask? But it's our only way out: finding, together, a territory we can live in.

This is the new universality. The only alternative is to pretend that nothing has changed, to withdraw behind our wall, and to continue to promote, with eyes wide open, the dream of the 'American way of life', while knowing that nine billion human beings will never benefit from it.

When everyone snuggles behind their fortifications, it is evidently the worst possible time to think in terms of the openness of borders and a revolution in lifestyles. However, migration and the new climate situation comprise *one and the same threat*.

Most of our fellow citizens deny what is happening to the Earth but understand perfectly well that the immigrant question will really put all of their desires for identity to the test. For now, encouraged by the so-called 'populist' parties, they have grasped ecological change in only one of its aspects: the fact that it is sending across their borders huge numbers of unwanted people. Hence their response: 'We must erect firm borders so we won't be swamped.'

But it's the other aspect of this same change that they still haven't properly realized: for a long time, the new climate situation has been sweeping away all borders, exposing us to every wind – and against such an invasion, we can build no walls.

If we wish to defend our identities, we are also going to have to identify those shapeless, stateless migrants known as climate, erosion, pollution, dwindling resources and the destruction of habitat. Even if you seal your borders against human refugees, you will never be able to stop these others getting through.

This is where we need to introduce an idea from science fiction – let's call it a plausible fiction.

The enlightened elites – they do exist – realized, after the 1990s, that the dangers summed up in the word 'climate' were increasing, though the word itself needs to be given a broad meaning: a new set of relations between human beings and the Earth, relations that had hitherto been quite stable. Until then, it had been possible to grab a piece of land, secure property rights over it, work it, and use it and abuse it – but the land itself kept more or less quiet.

The enlightened elites started to pile up evidence suggesting that this state of affairs wasn't going to last. They had known this for a long while, of course, but let's say they had bravely learned to ignore it. *Under* the soil of private property, the seizure of land, the working of territory, *another soil*, another land, another territory was starting to shift, to quake, to shake. A sort of earthquake, if you like, that really did start to shake up the enlightened elites. 'Look, nothing's going to be the same way as before; you're going to have to pay dearly for coming back to Earth and for a volte-face on the part of hitherto docile powers.'

The problem is that this threat, this warning, has been heard loud and clear by other elites who may be less enlightened but have plenty of money and large interests, and are above all extremely keen to ensure their own well-being.

And this is where the hypothesis of a political fiction intervenes: those elites have clearly understood that the warning was accurate, but they did not deduce from this undeniable truth that they would have to pay, and pay dearly, for the Earth to perform a volte-face on itself.

They drew two conclusions, both of which have now led to the election of a Lord of Misrule to the White House: yes, this volte-face needs to be paid for, at a high price, but it's *the others who will pay*, not us, no way; and this undeniable truth about the new climate situation is something *whose very existence we can deny.*

If this hypothesis is correct, it enables us to grasp what, from the 1980s, was called 'deregulation' and the 'dismantling of the Welfare State', from the 2000s, 'climate change denial', and above all, over the last forty years, a dizzying increase in inequality. And we need to see that all of these things are part of the same phenomenon: the elites were so thoroughly enlightened that they decided there would be no future life for the world, *so they needed to get rid of all the burdens of solidarity as fast as possible* (i.e. deregulation); that they needed to construct a kind of golden fortress for the few per cent of people who would manage to get on in life (i.e. soaring inequality); and that, to hide the crass selfishness of this flight from the common world, they would need to completely deny the very existence of the threat behind this mad dash (climate change denial). Without this hypothesis, we can't explain either the soaring inequality, or the scepticism about climate change, or the raging deregulation. These

three movements define the history into which continental
Europe finds it so difficult to fit.

Let's draw on the threadbare metaphor of the *Titanic*:
enlightened people can see the iceberg heading straight for the
prow, know that shipwreck is inevitable, grab the lifeboats,
and ask the orchestra to play enough lullabies so that they
can make a clean getaway under cover of night before the
alarming list of the vessel alerts the other classes!

Those people – the elites that we should now call, not
enlightened, but obscurantist – have realized that, if they
want to survive in comfort, *they shouldn't seem to be pre-
tending that they share their space with the rest of the world.*
Globalization immediately starts to look quite different: from
the ship's rails, the lower classes – who are now wide awake
– can see the lifeboats bobbing off into the distance. The
orchestra continues to play 'Nearer My God To Thee', but
the music is no longer enough to cover the howls of rage ...

And 'rage' is indeed the word to describe the reaction of
disbelief and bafflement that such an abandonment, such a
betrayal, arouses.

When political analysts try to grasp the current situation,
they use and abuse the term 'populism'. They accuse 'ordinary people' of indulging in a narrow-minded vision, in their
fears, their naive mistrust of elites, their bad taste in culture,
and above all in their passion for identity, folklore, archaism
and boundaries – let alone a culpable indifference to the facts.
These people lack generosity, open-mindedness, rationality;
they have no taste for risk (ah! that taste for risk, preached
by those who are safe wherever their air miles permit them
to fly).

This is to forget that 'ordinary folk' *have been callously
betrayed* by those who have abandoned the idea of truly
bringing about the modernization of the planet *with* everyone else, because they knew, before everyone else, better than
everyone else, that this modernization was impossible – for
lack of a planet big enough for their dreams of limitless
growth.

If Trump's election clarifies the new political situation, this
is because the horizon to which it is dragging the United States
gives an idea so *diametrically opposed* to the right direction
that it ultimately defines rather well, by way of contrast, the

nature of the third attractor! Indeed, Trump's innovation consists in setting out a whole political programme based on the systematic *denial* of climate change. For the first time, climate change denial is determining all political decisions. What a clarification!

We are failing to respect the originality of the fascists when we compare Trump with the movements of the 1930s. The only thing the two movements share is the invention of a new combination that, for a while, leaves the old elites completely disorientated. But the combinations invented by the different fascisms were still in line with the old vector, leading from ancient territories towards modernization. They managed to combine a return to a dreamed-of past – Rome, Germania – with revolutionary ideals and industrial and technical modernization, while reinventing the total state, the state at war *against* the very idea of the individual.

We find nothing of the kind in the current innovation: the state is mocked, the individual is king, and what needs to be done first and foremost is to save time by loosening all constraints – before everybody realizes that there is no world that corresponds to that America.

Trump's originality lies in the way he brings together, in one single movement, a mad dash for maximum profit while abandoning the rest of the world to its fate (the new members of his team responsible for 'ordinary folk' are billionaires!); a whole nation's mad dash backwards to national and ethnic categories ('Make America Great Again' – behind a wall!); and, finally, an explicit denial of the geological and climatic situation.

Trumpism – if we may use this term – is a political innovation of a kind we rarely see, and one that we need to take seriously. Just as fascism managed to combine extremes, to the complete surprise of the politicians and commentators of the time, Trumpism combines extremes and deceives the world with its trumpery, at least for a while. Instead of contrasting the two mad dashes – towards globalization and towards a return to the old national terrain – Trump acts as if they could be fused. This fusion is of course possible only if the very existence of a situation of conflict between modernization on the one hand and material conditions on the other is denied. Hence the role of climate-change scepticism, which cannot be understood without this. (Remember that, up until Clinton, questions of climate change could be agreed on by both parties.)

And it is easy to see why: the total lack of realism in the combination – billionaires encouraging millions of members of the so-called middle classes to return to protecting the past! – is blindingly self-evident. For now, it's nothing more than a matter of remaining completely indifferent to the *geo*political situation.

For the first time, a whole political movement is no longer claiming it can seriously confront geopolitical realities, but is explicitly placing itself outside of any constraint, 'offshore', as it were – as in tax havens. What counts most of all is that they should not have to share with the masses a world that, as they know, will never again be held in common. As if that third attractor, that spectre that is haunting the whole of politics, could be held at bay indefinitely.

It is quite remarkable that this invention comes from a real-estate developer who is forever in debt, going from one bankruptcy to another, and who became a celebrity thanks to reality TV (another form of unrealistic escapism). The complete indifference to facts that marked the electoral campaign as much as it marks the new administration is simply a consequence of claiming you can live without being grounded in reality. When you've promised those who think they're heading back to a country they once knew that they will indeed rediscover their past there (whereas you're actually dragging them towards a place that, for the great mass of electors, has no real existence), then you can't be too per-nickety about empirical evidence!

It's pointless to get angry when Trump's electors 'don't believe the facts': they're not stupid. The situation is quite the opposite: it's because the overall geopolitical situation has to be denied that an indifference to facts becomes so essential. If they had to realize what a huge contradiction there is between the mad dash forwards and the mad dash backwards, they'd have to start coming down to earth! In this sense, Trumpism defines (albeit negatively, of course, by taking up the opposite position) the first ecologist government.

And it goes without saying that 'ordinary folk' shouldn't have too many illusions about how the venture is going to

turn out. Those most attracted by Trump are exactly those
tiny elites who, at the beginning of the 1990s, detected that
there was no possible world that they could share with nine
billion individuals. 'Push deregulation to the limit, pump out
everything there's still left to pump out of the ground – drill,
baby, drill! – and if we follow Trump we'll end up winning
thirty or forty years' respite for us and our children. *Après
nous, le déluge* – we'll be dead anyway.'

Accountants are well acquainted with entrepreneurs who
behave in a 'cavalier' fashion towards the facts. Trump's
originality lies in the way he makes the greatest nation on
earth behave in a similarly cavalier way. Donald Trump: the
Bernie Madoff of the state! Not forgetting what lies behind
the whole situation: he is in charge of the nation that *has
the most to lose* from a return to reality, from a change of
direction towards the attractor Earth. It's a crazy decision to
make, but it's understandable.

You don't need to be very bright to foresee that the whole
thing will end in a terrible conflagration. This is the only real
parallel with the different fascisms. Marx was wrong: history
does not go simply from tragedy to farce, it can repeat itself
once more as a tragic piece of buffoonery.

In any case, the clarification that this innovation has produced gives *progressive forces* – defined now as those that
turn their attention to the third term, i.e. the Earth – a precise
idea of the difficulties they are going to have to face. It's no
longer enough to divert those dreaming of a return to their
homeland from their path; it's no longer enough to form
an alliance with those aiming at gaining access to a global
dimension: we now need to confront head-on those whom
the Pied Piper is leading in a direction that will take us, yet
again, away from the Earth.

Peter Sloterdijk once said that Europe was the club of
nations that had definitively abandoned the idea of empire.
Let's leave the Brexiteers, those who voted for Trump, the
Turks, the Chinese and the Russians to wallow in their
dreams of imperial domination. We know that, if they still
wish to reign over a territory in the cartographical sense of
the word, they have no more chance than we did of domi-
nating the Earth that, nowadays, dominates us as well as it
dominates them. So the challenge to be met is *tailor-made*

for Europe, since it is Europe that invented the strange story of globalization before becoming one of its victims. History belongs to those who can be the first to come to earth, to land on an earth that can be inhabited – unless the others, the dreamers of old-style *Realpolitik*, have finally made this earth vanish away for good.

Translated by Andrew Brown

8

Overcoming the fear of freedom

Paul Mason

Leigh, UK, 1976: It was the first time I ever heard the n-word in public. I was standing with my dad on the terraces at a rugby league match – among maybe four thousand people packed behind the goalposts. Our club had signed a black player and this was his first big game.

In the 1970s, fans from both teams always mixed together in the stands. But that day the away fans were being obnoxious. Every time our new player got the ball, a few of them started monkey chants. Some shouted: 'stupid nigger'. Worse, some of our own fans joined in. I was embarrassed and powerless. And then our new player picked up the ball, flattened three men in front of him, and scored.

I can still see my dad, and hear the complete silence around us, as he turned to the crowd, spread his arms wide and shouted at the top of his voice: 'So, what do you think of that "nigger" now?'

What gave one poorly educated white man the authority to morally defeat racism? My dad had no special status: he was not a union leader or a pub brawler. He was just one member of a working-class community prepared to call for adherence to its traditional values.

Leigh was not a radical town. There was, however, an intense and unspoken political culture: hatred for everything to do with the rich; mistrust of anything from outside;

suspicion of anyone whose behaviour seemed to place the logic of the market above human decency: salespeople, rent collectors, thieves.

Because so much of our capacity to resist lay in this exclusion of outsiders we understood that, if racism ever took hold among us, it would get vicious. When they met black people, miners of my dad's generation would always reassure them with a line from the Paul Robeson movie, *The Proud Valley*: 'Aren't we all black down that pit?' But nobody was prepared for the day the pit disappeared, together with the engineering factories, works football teams and social clubs.

When the 1980 recession started, and mass unemployment hit us, my dad, who'd been a boy in the 1930s, told me: 'if there's another Depression, racial prejudice will come back'. In the end, it did not need a Depression.

In 2016 the people of my town voted by two-to-one for Brexit. Though Labour still won all elections to the local borough council in that year, the right-wing racist party UKIP came second in half the wards, ousting the Conservatives as the main alternative to Labour. In the 2015 general election UKIP gained just under 9,000 votes out of 45,000 cast. Around 2,700 people had previously voted for the fascist British National Party in 2010, and those votes are now wrapped up inside UKIP's total. The town will be, for the foreseeable future, a target seat for the xenophobic right.

In the pubs and clubs, former miners and shop stewards try to hold the line: arguing for socialism and anti-racism, pinning the blame for poverty and stagnation on the rich, and on the policy of austerity. The problem is, even when they win, it is at a cost: the cost of tolerating open racism and xenophobia in the very spaces where it was unspeakable thirty years ago.

The culture of resistance to capital has, for some, mutated into a culture of revolt against globalization, migration and human rights. How we got here is not just a story of neo-liberalism's economic failure, but the collapse of a narrative. In turn, the paralysis of the left lies not in its failure to advance economic criticisms of free market economics, but in its failure to engage properly in the narrative battle the ultra-right is waging. Exploring this narrative battle in detail has nothing to do with the classic postmodernist thesis in which the sign precedes the signified thing. It has become a matter of life and death for social democracy.

The neoliberal attack

Neoliberalism announced itself through vindictive acts: Thatcher and Reagan in 1980/81 both used pro-cyclical economics to unleash the destruction of traditional industries, with the specific aim of atomizing the working class and destroying the effectiveness of trade unions.

Foucault had predicted we would become 'entrepreneurs of the self'.[1] But my father's generation had other ideas. To them, competition and behaviour motivated by commerce were taboo. They had to be taught to stab each other in the back during years of unemployment and humiliation in the welfare system. Or through work in factories that were suddenly unsafe, where unions were forbidden.

For neoliberalism this was a battle to impose a new narrative on millions of people's lives. A whole generation of workers was forced to behave as if the logic of the market was more important than the logic of place, or class identity – even if they did not believe this to be true.

Wages collapsed. Solidarity was eroded. The archetypal outsiders in our communities – the thief, the con-man, the rent collector, the strike-breaker – became the folk heroes of Thatcherism. They set up small companies: cleaning firms, security firms, suntan parlours, firms to train factory workers to write CVs. Around these firms organized crime flourished – so that, in the terraced streets where there had once been social order, the drug dealer, the sex worker and the loan shark became part of the landscape.

To be frank: it broke us. Some fought – like the miners, who went on strike for twelve months in 1984/5. But most broke without fighting. Instead, early on, working-class communities adopted a strategy of passive cultural resistance to neoliberalism outside work. In the workplace – where bullying and rampant exploitation now took off – people conformed to the new rituals, language and norms. But in the private and semi-social spaces – the family home, the social club, the pub – they spoke freely and nursed their grievances.

In the 1980s there emerged the beginnings of a working-class culture forcibly separated from work. Then, during the 1990s, it became a working-class culture remote from work, indifferent to work, and centred on a world beyond work.

By the early 1990s there was something to assuage the misery: credit. Pawn shops, last seen in the 1930s, reappeared: you could pawn your plastic stereo system, your Chinese-made guitar, your child's pram. Mortgages were readily available – not just for people who had worked and saved but for those who'd done neither. And credit cards were plentiful, even for idiots who routinely maxed out on them and then defaulted. Then the payday loan companies appeared, lending at 1,000 per cent interest. On top of that – with the entry of China into the market – globalization began significantly to reduce the cost of basic goods.

If life for working-class people felt better in the 1990s than the 1980s, it was because both credit and cheap Chinese goods offset the primary problem: stagnating wages. That globalization and financial deregulation are essentially positive for working people became the overt message of social democracy.

The moral effects of structural transformation

Neoliberalism unleashed numerous structural transformations. The principal ones were: the offshoring of productive industries; the restructuring of corporations into a 'value chain' of smaller companies; cutting taxes to shrink the state; the privatization of public services; and the financialization of everyday life. Only by understanding the narrative effects of these changes, as well as their direct economic effects, can we understand the ideological collapse of centrism that has begun in 2016.

Offshoring of production was designed to reduce wage costs and reduce the wage share of GDP. In Leigh, the most significant industry to be moved offshore was Coles Cranes, a big engineering firm, whose parent company collapsed. But

the wider narrative effect was, as David Harvey has put it, to
'annihilate space': to signal to an entire class that *place – the
key source of your identity – does not matter.*

The *restructuring* of firms into segments producing different rates of profit was done in order to subject all aspects of
corporate life to the dictates of the financial markets. Now,
maintaining a social club and a bowling green (both existed
in the local factory I worked at in 1979) was no longer
logical. You could still have a canteen, provided now by an
outsourced catering firm, but it had to make a profit. The
signalling effect of this was equally clear: *that the firm would
no longer carry any informal social obligations.*

The third big structural reform was to *slash progressive
taxation.* The aim was – ideologically – to shrink the size
of the state. But once the asset bubbles began, and offshore
tax havens mushroomed, the secondary impact of low taxation was to increase inequality and suppress social mobility. At a signalling level, the erosion of the welfare state,
and of free public services, told the working class that *the
post-1945 social bargain was over.* Only those parts of
the welfare state that were functional for capital would be
retained.

Privatization, the fourth weapon of neoliberalism, renewed
the stock of profit-generating capital, and cured the profits
crisis that had plagued the late Keynesian era. Toll roads, rail
privatizations, the chaotic fragmentation of local bus services,
the new power to terminate electricity and gas supplies for the
poor ... – these things were done to make public services as
expensive as possible. Their narrative effect was to erode the
concept of a public economic realm: henceforward it became
logical to plan your life as if only yourself and your close
family, not the state and wider community, would be there
to catch you if you fell. Combined with Thatcher's termina-
tion of the public housebuilding programme, the message to
working-class families was clear: *You are on your own. The
state is not actually here to help you but to make all public
services as expensive and scarce as possible.*

Finally, the *financialization* of consumption was just part
of the wider financialization of capitalism itself. All firms
were now dictated their priorities by the analyst class in
the investment banks. Sentimental managers who wanted to

maintain the social partnership rituals they had learned in
the 1960s and 1970 were ousted. And this was the biggest
cultural signal of all. In future, the highest status would
be awarded not to the local boss, still on first name terms
with shop stewards. *Instead, Thatcherism would celebrate
the egomaniac of the trading floor.* And unlike with the
mid-twentieth-century bourgeoisie, which was impenetrable,
a pushy, egotistical working-class person could become part
of this new entrepreneurial elite.

By celebrating the financial predator as a new kind of working
-class hero, neoliberalism began to repackage 'working-class
culture' as a pro-capitalist ideology, celebrating ignorance and
egotism – that is, precisely the opposite of what it had been.
If you compare any episode from the soap opera *Coronation
Street* in the 1960s to its rival *EastEnders*, which began in the
Thatcher era, you can observe – albeit through the prism of
clichéd writing – the moral impact of neoliberalism. Instead
of the calm and rational language of the 1960s, there was
now shouting, the slamming of doors, fists waved in the faces
of women, suicide, depression – and the ever present fear of
drugs and burglary. Addiction, anger and dependency controlled these new dramatic archetypes like the gods control
the characters in a Greek drama. They had lost agency and
complexity; they had become two-dimensional social cyphers
and the servants of fate.

Whereas for my father's generation everything in the system
worked to oxygenate anti-racism, internationalism and self-
educated altruism, neoliberalism now pumped oxygen to
their opposites.[2] And for three decades the function of this
was to disrupt and disaggregate working-class resistance to
neoliberalism. The problem is, when neoliberalism itself collapsed, it was no longer mainstream conservatism that got
oxygenated, but authoritarian right-wing populism.

The narrative failure of neoliberalism

Neoliberalism failed by stages. By the late 1990s its promise
of social mobility was clearly broken. By the early 2000s
the dotcom crash and corporate scandals like Equitable
Life had begun to close off access to the company pension

system, into which the upper third of the workforce had contributed.

As offshoring created more and more ex-industrial communities entirely reliant on public sector work and welfare, Labour signalled it would do nothing to slow the pace of change; nor would it protect the old forms of social cohesion. At the 2005 Labour Party conference Tony Blair warned that debating globalization was like debating whether autumn should follow summer: 'The character of this changing world is indifferent to tradition. Unforgiving of frailty. No respecter of past reputations. It has no custom and practice. It is replete with opportunities, but they only go to those swift to adapt, slow to complain, open, willing and able to change.'

It was a clear, final call on the ex-industrial working class to give up the last, eviscerated vestiges of their culture. In its place Blair and Gordon Brown staked everything on financialization. Deregulation of the credit market would allow even the poor to take part in the asset-price bubble. The booming finance industry would generate high tax revenues, which would be redistributed to the working class through welfare payments, in-work tax credits, revived spending on the NHS, and mass access to university education. On the eve of the financial crash up to seven million people, one third of all households, were receiving some form of payment from the state.

When the finance system collapsed, so did this finance-based ameliorative project of social democracy. In its place came austerity. Austerity capped health and welfare spending. Through punitive benefit withdrawals it forced so many families to rely on food banks that the main charity running them gave out 1.1 million emergency parcels a year. It withdrew sickness and disability benefits from one million former workers below retirement age. And as the safety net broke, so did consent for inward migration.

How consent for migration disintegrated

Britain – like the US, Germany and France – had absorbed millions of migrants in the post-war era. The crude racism of a minority of white, conservative workers was assuaged through migrants integrating with British culture. White workers turned towards fascism only in small numbers, and in a form so violent it was easily suppressed. As a result, in the major cities, the actual working class was, by the 1980s, indelibly multi-ethnic: African-Caribbeans, Muslims, Hindus, Somalis – all started out marginalized; all experienced racism. And all can now be found everywhere in the typical workplace of the city: the transport system, the hospital, the supermarket till and the software house.

The accession to the EU of ten East European (A10) countries completely changed this dynamic. In two stages (excluding Romania and Bulgaria at first) the British government enthusiastically encouraged people from Eastern Europe to take up their rights under the free movement of people embodied in the Treaty of the European Union.

Since the 1970s, consent for migration had been maintained by heavily controlling the inward flow – from Kenya, India or Bangladesh. In contrast, the East European migrants arrived by right, not permission. They would never be citizens: by 2016 there were three million of them, but they could not vote in a general election.

Secondly, East European migration was specifically designed to suppress wages and conditions, even if the general macroeconomic outcomes barely registered this effect. The East European migrant workforce mapped perfectly onto the new institutions of precarious work. And in the 'Viking' and 'Laval' cases at the European Court of Justice, the right of employers to 'post' low-paid workforces from one country to another was established.

A third change was that, while black and Asian migration had flowed into the cities, East European migration flowed into small-town communities where there was almost no prior experience of migration; where there were few of the resilient networks that allow multi-ethnic cities to function; and where pressure on public services was already high. And East European migration sent another narrative signal to the existing UK working class: this is the kind of worker we prefer – *flexible, silent, pliant, deferential, without rights, contributing little to the wider demos and expecting nothing back.*

Neoliberalism's defence of the freedom of movement was first of all fatalistic: it is a 'fact' of modern life that cannot be controlled or countermanded. Then, when studies did begin to show wage suppression at the bottom end of the labour market, this was deemed to be marginal and insignificant, and offset by the wider macroeconomic gains. When they noticed how unsettled UK-born workers were becoming over the pressure migration placed on services, the centre left assumed this could be offset by promising to vector in cash to the affected places, not bothering to address the objection that the cash would have to come from somewhere else.

Neoliberalism assumed it could overcome anti-migrant hostility because for thirty years it had been annihilating space, individuality and locale. Globalization was a natural process, unstoppable, and people would eventually acquiesce, as they had done in all the other structural reforms. Instead, it created a revolt of the working poor in Britain that has caused the first crack in the multilateral framework of the global system: Brexit.

The 52 per cent vote for Brexit was not driven only by white workers: 27 per cent of black people and 33 per cent of Asians voted Leave according to one exit poll. And 59 per cent of all Leave voters were upper or middle class. But the strongest Leave votes took place in small-town Britain, where the residue of working-class culture had now turned into an 'identity' whose main characteristic was defiance: not just of globalization but of the liberal, transnational, human-rights-based culture that it has fostered.

Strikingly, this fake rebellion of the poor was then able to exert upward hegemony into the middle class of small towns. Being a professional was a predictor of voting Remain in the cities, but not in small ex-industrial towns. Since the vote, numerous middle-class people have admitted: 'though I wanted to vote Remain, I understood why poor people were hurting and for their sake voted to Leave'.

Only by understanding the source of anger can you defuse it. The anger of UK-born workers, black and white, was more against the migration system than migrants themselves. It was, and remains, the ultimate symbol of neoliberalism's desire to annihilate space, community and non-abstract labour. Isolating and defeating the racism of the authoritarian populist right-wing worker cannot be done through econom-ics alone; it requires a battle to reassert a social-democratic plebeian identity, within a networked and individualistic world.

The narrative struggle ahead

It has been clear since 2008 that, unless we abandon neo-liberalism, globalization will fall apart. With Brexit and the election of Donald Trump that process has now begun.

The fatal attraction neoliberalism exerted on the elite, and on two generations of professional economists, was rooted in its apparent perfection. In its economic content it confirmed the notion that capitalism is essentially the market, survival of the fittest, and the small state. In its political form it fitted perfectly the core liberal-democratic assumption: that we are all merely citizens, not workers or bosses, and that all our rights are primarily individual, not collective. Even now – with Renzi fallen, Hollande stumbling to the end of his presidency, Schäuble demanding yet more austerity in Greece – the social and political elite of neoliberalism has barely begun to question this essentialist mindset. Instead a break has begun in the opposite direction. The authoritarian populism that is mobilizing a minority of working-class voters across Europe is, essentially, a demand for de-globalization. Its reactionary nature lies not only in its preference for racism, Islamophobia and social conservatism but in its complete ignorance of the complexity of the task.

In contrast to the 1930s, economic nationalism today has to dismantle a complex, organic and resilient system. It may shatter easily – through a currency war or a series of massive debt write-offs – but if so it will make cities in the countries on the losing side look like New Orleans after Hurricane Katrina.

Fortunately, the mass political demographics point in a completely different direction than in the 1930s. The individualist and liberated behaviours and beliefs detested by the xenophobic ultra-right are firmly embedded into an entire generation. According to YouGov, in the UK, though around 19 per cent of people hold strong right-wing and 29 per cent hold centrist 'authoritarian populist' beliefs, the biggest group – at 37 per cent – is the 'pro-EU, internationalist liberal left'.[3]

Modern society is no Weimar Republic, where tolerance and multiculturalism existed as a thin skin covering reactionary, hierarchical and nationalist mindsets. The new behaviours, beliefs, levels of tolerance, attachment to human rights and their universality, are the product of both technological change and education. They would have to be torn by force out of the minds, bodies and microstructures of most people under the age of thirty-five.

I have argued elsewhere[4] that the industrial proletariat not only failed in its resistance to neoliberalism in the 1980s but has, as a result of the technological revolution, been supplanted as the agent of social change by a more amorphous group described by sociologists like Manuel Castells as consisting of 'networked individuals'. These include not only the lower strata of the professional class and students but large parts of the ordinary workforce: the nurse, the barista, the software geek. Even what is left of the securely employed industrial workforce is, by virtue of the norms of the hi-tech manufacturing workplace, largely plugged in to this globalist culture.

In this sense, the networked individual is 'the working class sublated'. If there is a collective agent of history to drive the transition beyond capitalism then it is the young, networked, relatively liberated human being. They are not a class – though they are largely dispossessed of an economic future by neoliberalism's collapse. But if we insert them into the 1930s scenario as a parallel, the potential for a positive outcome becomes clear.

Writing about the rise of fascism, Erich Fromm concluded that it was being driven not just by economic grievances but by a 'fear of freedom'. An authoritarian mindset among the German petit bourgeoisie and some workers made them react to their own powerlessness through the 'desire to be dominated'. Fromm writes that though there was strong resistance to Nazism from both the organized workers and the liberal and Catholic bourgeoisie, this collapsed. First, because of 'a state of inner tiredness and resignation'.[5] Second, because of the material legacy of the defeats German workers suffered between 1919 and 1923. Finally because, beginning around 1930, the ideologies of resistance became exhausted.

Today, faced with Trump, Brexit and the disintegration of the global order, it is the neoliberal centrist political elite that is suffering feelings of resignation and disbelief. The vital tasks for the networked individual demographic are to engage and ally with the internationalists among small-town working-class communities, to nurture what is left of the narrative that allowed my dad's generation to shout down racism, and to fuse this with a narrative of hope about the future.

The task for social democracy is not to assuage the conservative desires of populist authoritarians. It is to project a confident alternative that fits the needs and the passions of the networked, educated plebeian majority of the workforce. This means a conscious reversal of the tactical assumptions behind 'Third Way' politics. Blair, Clinton, Schröder, Renzi – all assumed the manual working class of small towns would always vote left, and that social democracy had to appeal to the middle-class centre.

The collapse of neoliberalism, and the long erosion of working-class culture's progressive core, has to turn those assumptions upside down. A social democracy committed to human rights, gender equality, personal freedom and the protection of migrants and refugees has to regard its new core as including: the salariat of the big cities; the networked youth; the public sector workforce; the hi-tech and globalist workforce of the big corporations. Plus of course the ethnic minorities, migrant workers and women.

A renewed and radicalized social democracy cannot compromise with the reactionary mindset that has possessed around 20 per cent of voters in the place I was born. But it can offer them economic hope. It can offer them above all money – borrowed, taxed from the rich or printed by the central bank – to invest in schools, homes, jobs, public transport and healthcare. It is now common to hear die-hard plebeian racists pledge on phone-in programmes that they would rather see their economy destroyed and growth collapse than remain in the EU and accept migration. They have, in fact, grasped correctly what is at stake. But they, their families and their communities are about to find out you cannot eat racism.

The left's failure – and here I include the radical left such as Syriza and Podemos as well as the failing social democrats

– was to underestimate the fragility of the neoliberal narrative. Once one part of it was gone, the whole of it no longer made sense. Though we have critiqued the economic content of neoliberalism, we have tended to map our own narrative onto the assumed permanence of its political forms. Now the left has to fight right-wing nationalism in working-class communities by telling a different story.

Neoliberalism replaced the old story of collaboration and cohesion with a story about individuals. They were abstract people with abstract rights: the name badge on their uniforms was only for the benefit of the customer or the boss, not for the expression of their identity. The workers of the defeated and left-behind communities clung to what was left of their collective identity. But since its driving utopia – socialism – had been declared impossible by everybody including the socialist parties, they began to centre that identity on what was left: on accent, place, family and ethnicity.

Since 2008, though they have prevented the Depression my father's generation feared, central bank policies and state intervention have created a tendency towards stagnation: the 'low growth, low inflation, low interest rate equilibrium' described by Bank of England chief Mark Carney at the G20 in March 2016. But there cannot be equilibrium in these circumstances, particularly where the medicine of austerity requires continued attacks on the welfare systems and wages on which low-income communities rely.

As long as neoliberalism told a coherent story, those who were its biggest victims – the low-skilled working class in ex-industrial towns – could survive, albeit with a strong, privately expressed identity of their own. But between 2008 and 2016 the allure of the neoliberal story waned – and faster than even its critics imagined. In this we are going through a moment analogous to the one that happened in Russia during Perestroika.

In the late 1980s, under Gorbachev, many Russians experienced a sudden 'break in consciousness', as the realization dawned that the fall was imminent. But until then most people behaved, spoke and even thought as if the Soviet system were permanent. And despite their cynicism about its brutality, many went on parades and performed the rituals demanded by the state. The Russian anthropologist Alexei

Yurchak describes these events in a book whose title speaks for itself: *Everything Was Forever, Until It Was No More.*

Since Trump's victory it has become possible to believe a similar collapse will happen in the West – of globalization, liberal social values, human rights and the rule of law. If so, the default form of capitalism will become, from Moscow to Washington, a xenophobic, oligarchic nationalism. If that happens, all projects for social justice and human liberation would have to be recalibrated on a national scale, just as they were in the 1930s.

But it is avoidable. In the next phase, the project of the left should be to save globalization by ditching neoliberalism. Specifically – as Carney has now suggested – we need new mechanisms to suppress inequality and redistribute the proceeds of trade and technological progress towards workers and young people. To do this we need to partially reverse the five structural reforms described above:

- Adopt industrial policies that bring productive jobs back to the global north, regardless of its effects on GDP per capita growth in the global south.
- Force corporations to accept their social duties towards real, concrete and specific communities, not civil society in the abstract.
- Renationalize key public services in order to provide them cheap or free, ameliorating the effects of precarious work.
- Eradicate offshore tax structures and the shadow banking system, bringing billions of taxable wealth onshore, in order to pay for massive, rapid and life-enhancing increases in public investment.
- De-financialize the economy: raising wages, reducing credit dependency, stabilizing both public and private sector debts through write-offs, controlled inflation and, where needed, capital controls.

These measures would not kill globalization. But they would reverse it in part; they would stabilize and save what we can of the globally interconnected economy, but at the price of halting globalization, rolling it back under controlled conditions, always with an eye to resuming progress once the social imbalances are corrected. If GDP growth in the developing world becomes more equitable, and therefore slows down, that is a subordinate issue for the populations of the global north.

Long before the combined effects of these measures kick in, they could make an immediate impact if they simply became a coherent task list in the minds of millions of people – just as the raw Keynesianism of Roosevelt's New Deal did in the 1930s.

As to migration, in a world of mobile phones, the internet and organized crime it is impossible to stop without adopting the murderous measures that haunt the fantasies of the alt-right: electrified fences, suspension of international law, state-sanctioned murder at the border. The OECD has estimated that the US and the EU each have to absorb fifty million migrants between now and 2060 to avoid growth slowing towards zero.[6] So it is necessary to revive consent for inward migration by (a) directing it, monitoring it and allocating resources to the places where it impacts negatively on public services; (b) introducing labour market reforms that prevent employers utilizing a rootless, non-citizen migrant population as the ideal 'abstract worker'; (c) reversing austerity. A gear change from austerity to investment-driven growth would not only, in a matter of months, lessen competition for housing, healthcare and school places. It would also create a positive sum game, completely reframing the migration debate.

With Trump and Brexit it is time to move beyond the economic critique of neoliberalism. The most concrete political and economic challenge for the left is to construct the post-neoliberal narrative. All parties, all politicians, all structures, all theories which stand in the way of that should be discarded. For time is against us.

Notes

1 Michel Foucault, *The Birth of Biopolitics*, Basingstoke: Palgrave Macmillan, 2004, p. 226.
2 I am indebted to the novelist Jim Crace for suggesting the term 'oxygenation' here.
3 Joe Twyman, 'Trump, Brexit, Front National, AfD: Branches of the Same Tree', 16 November 2016, at https://yougov.co.uk/

news/2016/11/16/trump-brexit-front-national-afd-branches-same-tree (retrieved November 2016).

4 See my book *Postcapitalism: A Guide to Our Future*, London: Allen Lane, 2015.

5 Erich Fromm, *Escape From Freedom*, New York: Henry Holt, 1994, p. 207.

6 Henrik Braconier, Giuseppe Nicoletti and Ben Westmore, 'Policy Challenges for the Next 50 Years' (2014), OECD Economic Policy Papers 9, at http://www.oecd.org/economy/Policy-challenges-for-the-next-fifty-years.pdf (retrieved November 2016).

9

Politics in the age of resentment: the dark legacy of the Enlightenment

Pankaj Mishra

The political earthquakes of our times – whether the triumph of Donald Trump, a self-confessed sexual predator and racist, the electoral apotheosis in India and the Philippines of strongmen accused of mass murder (Narendra Modi and Rodrigo Duterte), or the mass acclaim in Russia and Turkey for such pitiless despots and imperialists as Vladimir Putin and Recep Tayyip Erdoğan – have revealed an enormous pent-up energy. The near-simultaneous rise of demagoguery across the world points to a shared, codetermining situation, even though the secessions of our time, from ISIS to Brexit, have many local causes. For one, ethical constraints have weakened everywhere, often under the pressure of public opinion. What used to be called 'Muslim rage', and identified with mobs of brown-skinned men with bushy beards, is suddenly manifest globally, from saffron-robed Buddhist ethnic-cleansers in Myanmar to blonde white nationalists in Germany. As Freud wrote, the 'primitive, savage and evil impulses of mankind have not vanished' but continue to exist in a 'repressed state', waiting for 'opportunities to display their activity'.[1]

How do we understand this near-universal breakdown, which seems as much moral and emotional as political? Our concepts and categories derived from three decades of economistic liberalism seem unable to absorb an explosion of uncontrolled forces: for one, the 'masses' suddenly seem a lot more malleable and unpredictable than we had assumed. Consequently, confusion and bewilderment marks many political, business and media elites. *The Economist*, a reliable vendor of *bien pensant* thinking among these chosen people, has lurched lately from indignation over 'post-truth politics' (a false claim in itself) to the Rip Van Winkleish announcement of a 'New Nationalism'. Publications like *Vanity Fair* read as parodies of the *New Left Review* as they attend belatedly to the fiascos of global capitalism: most egregiously, its failure to fulfil its own promise of general prosperity and its contempt for the democratic principle of equality.

Well-worn pairs of rhetorical opposites – progressive-reactionary, fascism-liberalism, rational-irrational – have again been put to work. But, as a scattered intellectual industry plays catch-up with fast-moving events and the flowing meanings of human actions, it is hard not to suspect that our search for rational political alternatives to the current disorder may be fatally compromised. For whether they are left-leaning, centrist or rightist, opponents of the new political 'irrationalism' are still inhibited by the assumption that individuals are rational actors, motivated by material self-interest, enraged by its frustration, and, therefore, likely to be appeased by its fulfilment.

This is a notion of human motivation originally developed during the Enlightenment, which, despising tradition and religion, posited as their modern substitute the human capacity to rationally identify individual and collective interests. In its explanatory schema, assumed by those on the left as well as the right of the ideological spectrum, the self-seeking bourgeois, or *Homo economicus*, is the human norm, a freely willing subject whose natural desires and instincts are shaped by his ultimate motivation: to pursue happiness and avoid pain. This simple view always neglected many factors ever-present in human lives: the fear, for instance, of losing honour, dignity and status; the distrust of change; the appeal of stability and familiarity. There was no place in it for more complex drives: vanity, fear of appearing vulnerable, or 'image-making'. Obsessed with material progress, the hyper-rationalists ignored, too, the lure of the identity conferred by 'backwardness' and the tenacious pleasures of victimhood.

Our own disregard of these non-economic motivations seems more astonishing when we remember how the Enlightenment's 'narrow rational programme' for individual happiness had become by the late nineteenth century, as Robert Musil wrote in 1922, the 'butt of ridicule and contempt'.[2] Indeed, most modernist literature, philosophy and art is defined by its insistence that there is more to human beings than rational egoism, competition and acquisition; more to society than a contract between logically calculating and autonomous individuals; and more to politics than impersonal technocrats devising hyper-rational schemes of progress with the help of polls, surveys, statistics, mathematical models and technology. Beyond the simplest worldly transaction lies the vast realm of the unconscious. The intellect entrusted with rational calculations is, as Freud wrote, 'a feeble and dependent thing, a plaything and tool of our impulses and emotions'.[3]

The stunning revolutions of our time, and our perplexity before them, make it imperative that we anchor thought again in the sphere of impulses and emotions; these upheavals demand nothing less than a radically expanded understanding of what it means to be human. Such a journey, which was first undertaken a century ago, necessarily takes us far beyond liberalism and its supposed antidotes of equitable economic growth and distribution. We cannot do better in our own post-communist and *post-liberal* era than begin with the frank admission that Michael Ignatieff, a self-described liberal internationalist, recently made in an essay on the Marxist thinker Perry Anderson, that 'Enlightenment humanism and a historical vision' can't 'explain the world we're living in'.[4]

This is, by any measure, a massive intellectual failure. For the liberal Enlightenment ideal of a universal commercial society was never more fully realized than during the last two decades of hectic globalization. In the nineteenth century, Marx could still sneer at Jeremy Bentham for taking 'the modern shopkeeper, especially the English shopkeeper, as the normal man'.[5] In our own time, however, the ideology of neoliberalism, a reified form of Enlightenment rationalism and nineteenth-century utilitarianism, achieved near-total domination in economic and political realms, especially after the discrediting of its socialist rival in 1989.

The success of neoliberalism can be attested by many innovations of recent decades that now look perfectly naturalized. The growth of GDP is the irreplaceable index of national power and wealth; individual freedom is conflated with consumer choice; the market is expected to supply valuable products and services while the task of governments is restricted to ensuring fair competition. Market-based indices of success and failure have come to dictate even academic and cultural life.

The broader intellectual revolution accompanying neoliberalism has been no less sweeping. The collapse of communism, the illegitimate child of Enlightenment rationalism and humanism, encouraged Op-Ed writers as well as politicians and businessmen to assume that Western-style democracy and capitalism had solved the modern riddle of injustice and inequality. In this utopian vision, a global economy built around free markets, competition and individual entrepreneurship would alleviate ethnic and religious differences and usher in worldwide prosperity and peace, and any irrational obstacles to the spread of liberal modernity, such as Islamic fundamentalism, would eventually be eradicated.

Today, however, this post-Cold War consensus lies in ruins. Fanatics and bigots have been empowered in the very heart of the modern West following the most sustained experiment in enlightened self-interest, maximizing happiness and free-marketeering. Thomas Piketty may be right to argue that 'Trump's victory is primarily due to the explosion in economic and geographic inequality in the United States.'[6] But many rich men and women, not to mention African-Americans and Hispanics, also voted for a compulsive groper; the prospering classes of India, Turkey, Poland and the Philippines remain steadfastly loyal to their increasingly volatile demagogues. The new representatives of the left-behinds and the downtrodden – Trump and Nigel Farage in a gold-plated lift, the founder of ISIS wearing a Rolex, and Modi in a personalized Savile Row suit – speak of an expanded theatre of political absurdism.

Gary Younge is right to warn 'that the link between economic anxiety and rightwing nationalism can be overdone'.[7] Mike Davis speaking of nihilist passions – that some people 'wanted change in Washington at any price, even if it meant

putting a suicide bomber in the Oval Office'[8] – is echoed by
Barack Obama, who thinks that Trump made an irresistible
'argument that he would blow this place up'. Certainly, voters
defying pseudo-rational pollsters and data-analysing pundits
around the world have come to resemble Dostoevsky's Underground Man, the quintessential loser dreaming of revenge
against his society's winners.

Writing in the 1860s, during the high noon of nineteenth-
century liberalism, Dostoevsky was one of the first to air
the suspicion, now troubling us, that rational thinking does
not decisively influence human behaviour. He pitted his
Underground Man against the then popular idea in Russia,
imported by eager readers of John Stuart Mill and Bentham,
of rational egoism, or material self-interest. Dostoevsky's pro-
tagonist obsessively assaults the shared positivist assumption
of both capitalists and socialists, that human beings are logically calculating animals:

> Oh, tell me who was it first announced, who was it first pro-
> claimed that man only does nasty things because he does not
> know his own interests; and that if he were enlightened, if his
> eyes were opened to his real normal interests, man would at
> once cease to do nasty things, would at once become good
> and noble because, being enlightened and understanding to
> his real advantage, he would see his own advantage in the
> good and nothing else?[9]

Dostoevsky defined a style of thought later elaborated by
Nietzsche, Freud, Weber and Musil, to name but a few of
the 'masters of suspicion', in what came to be a full-blown
intellectual revolt against the confident certainties of ratio-
nalist ideologies, liberal, democratic or socialist. Musil, an
engineer by training, was by no means a propagandist for
the neo-romantic cults and blood-and-soil nationalisms of
his time. The problem, as he saw it, is not that 'we have
too much intellect and too little soul', but rather that we
have 'too little intellect in matters of the soul'.[10] Most other
writers and thinkers of the fin de siècle, who aimed to go
beyond the apparently real and the rational, also brought a
high degree of intellectual precision to their analysis of the
complex drivers of human action. In the process, they freshly

scrutinized the role of not only the repressed and obscure in private life but also of the hidden operators in the social and political life of liberal democracy. One gets the impression, Freud wrote in *The Future of an Illusion* (1927), 'that culture is something imposed on a reluctant majority by a minority that managed to gain possession of the instruments of power and coercion'.[11]

The works of art, literature and philosophy that emerged from the complex new definition of human subjectivity posited even everyday consciousness (most famously in *Ulysses*) as marked by a series of vagrant journeys: into an irrepressible and often painful past, an elusive present, and a future beset with unknown risks. All human action, in the modernist view, inevitably takes place at a distance from its professed principles and ideals; there is an irreducible gap between theory and practice, where fear, hope, vanity, anger and vengeance lurk. What we call the 'self' is a dynamic entity, constantly shaped and re-shaped in the interplay between what Freud termed the 'psychic apparatus' and historically developing social and cultural conditions.

In this sense, neither today's 'raging' Muslims nor alt-rightists are irredeemable fanatics and racists. They do not have a fixed self – as distinct from projections of fears, desires and aspirations that, like all things human, are constantly being undone by their own contradictions. This is why their ostensibly racial or religious resentments cannot be adequately grasped by close readings of the Koran or Breitbart News. They are best understood through the interplay of the irreducibly divided human self with its social, political and cultural context.

What distinctively marks the latter today, and makes for much torment and conflict in the self, is a paradox: the fact that while the ideals of modern democracy have never been more popular, they have become progressively difficult, if not impossible, to realize under the conditions of neoliberal globalization. Tocqueville had noticed a troubling complex of emotions breeding in the first great democratic revolution of the United States. He worried that the New World's promise of meritocracy and 'equality of conditions' would make for immoderate ambition, corrosive envy and chronic dissatisfaction. In certain epochs, the passion for equality would

swell 'to the height of fury' and lead many to acquiesce in
a curtailment of their liberties, and to long for strongmen.[12]

We witness a universal frenzy of fear and loathing today
because the democratic revolution Tocqueville witnessed has
spread to the remotest corners of the world. The rage for
equality is conjoined with the pursuit of prosperity man-
dated by the global consumer economy, aggravating tensions
and contradictions in inner lives that are then played out in
the public sphere. 'To live in freedom', Tocqueville warned,
'one must grow used to a life full of agitation, change and
danger.'[13] This kind of life is appallingly barren of stability,
security, identity and honour, even when it overflows with
material goods. Nevertheless, it is now commonplace among
all those people around the globe that rational considerations
of utility and profit uproot, humiliate and render obsolete.

This widespread experience of modernity as maelstrom has
heightened the lure of *ressentiment*, an existential resentment
of other people's being, caused by an intense mix of envy and
a sense of humiliation and powerlessness, which, as it lingers
and deepens, poisons civil society and undermines political
liberty. *Ressentiment*, a compound of emotions, most clearly
reveals the human self in its fundamentally unstable relations
with the external world. Rousseau understood it profoundly,
even though he never used the word. As he saw it, people
in a commercial society live neither for themselves nor for
their country; they live for the satisfaction of their vanity,
or *amour-propre* – the desire and need to secure recognition
from others, to be esteemed by them as much as one esteems
oneself.

But this vanity, luridly exemplified by Donald Trump's
Twitter account, is doomed to be perpetually unsatisfied.
It is just too commonplace and parasitic on fickle opinion.
It ends up nourishing in the soul a dislike of one's own self
while stoking impotent hatred of others; and it can quickly
degenerate into an aggressive drive, whereby individuals feel
acknowledged only by being preferred over others, and by
rejoicing in their abjection.

Ressentiment breeds in proportion to the spread of the
ideals of a commercial and democratic society. In the early
twentieth century, the German sociologist Max Scheler built
a systematic theory of *ressentiment* as a characteristically

modern phenomenon, inherent in societies where formal
social equality between individuals coexists with massive differences in power, education, status and property ownership.
Such disparities now exist everywhere, along with expanded
notions of individual aspiration and equality. During the
neoliberal age, longings for wealth, status and power blos-
somed in the most unpromising circumstances; and equality
of conditions, in which talent, education and hard work are
rewarded by individual mobility, ceased to be an exclusively
American illusion after the end of the Cold War in 1989. The
fantasy of equality proliferated even as structural inequality entrenched itself further. Accordingly, *ressentiment* has
moved from being a European or American malady to a
global epidemic.

It incubates faster as the egalitarian ideals of democracy
collide with the neoliberal ideals of private wealth creation,
and transnational corporates and individuals secede from
the nation-state. Rational programmes for generating more
wealth through networked cities, or achieving a fairer society
through the 'sharing economy', fail to acknowledge that most
individuals today exist within either states with weakening
sovereignties or various poorly imagined social and political
collectivities. They not only suffer from the fact that, as Tocqueville wrote in another context, old certitudes about their
place in the world have been lost along with their links to
traditional communities and systems of support. Their social
isolation has also been intensified in many countries by the
decline of social democracy and postcolonial nation-building
programmes.

Indeed, neoliberalism has made disconnection from the
larger collectivity seem a requisite for private growth and
self-aggrandizement. The new individuals are now truly
condemned to be free even as they are enslaved further by
finely integrated political, economic and cultural powers: the
opaque workings of finance capital; the harsh machinery of
social security, juridical and penal systems; and the ideological pressures of educational institutions, the media and the
internet. Not surprisingly, there has been an exponential rise
in the number of people finding scapegoats among women
and minorities, or just someone to abuse on Twitter. These
apparent racists and misogynists have clearly suffered silently

for a long time from what Camus, presenting Scheler's definition of *ressentiment*, called 'the evil secretion, in a sealed vessel, of prolonged impotence'.[14] It was this ooze, a kind of gangrenous disease in social organisms, festering openly for long in the *Daily Mail* and Fox News, that erupted volcanically with Trump's victory.

Rich and poor alike voting for a serial liar and tax dodger have confirmed yet again that human desires operate independently of the logic of self-interest, and can be destructive of it. Indeed, we find ourselves at the eerily familiar conjuncture at which militantly disaffected masses in the late nineteenth century began to fall for radical alternatives to a harrowingly prolonged experiment in rational politics and economy.

Much of the early twentieth century's history has been related as a cautionary tale about how the manipulation of the mass unconscious by demagogues, and a cannily instrumentalized understanding of crowd psychology and mass media, contributed to the making of genocidal regimes and two world wars. But it is also true that the devastating failures of rational liberalism paved the way for hyper-rational totalitarian solutions. Stalin's Russia with its ultra-modern socioeconomic and cultural engineering was, as the historian Stephen Kotkin wrote, the 'quintessential Enlightenment utopia'.[15]

So shattering were the traumas inflicted by Nazism and Stalinism that, in an ironic twist of fate, they helped rehabilitate liberalism after 1945. It is, in fact, crucial to grasp that liberalism, tainted by its ruinous fiascos, received a fresh intellectual varnish during the stand-off of the Cold War. Swearing by the Enlightenment, Anglo-American liberals staunchly identified the non-communist West with benign rationality, branding its opponents as lethally irrational – an intellectual reflex recently demonstrated by laptop warriors against radical Islamism.

Like Stalinism, Nazism emerged, as Adorno and Horkheimer asserted, from the dialectic of the Enlightenment; and a racist British imperialism was, Hannah Arendt and Simone Weil argued, their true predecessor. Nevertheless, the ideologues of the free world suppressed the embarrassing continuities between their rationalism and other people's irrationalism as they claimed a high moral ground for themselves. During the Cold War, oppositions between the rational West and the irrational East, the Enlightenment and the Counter-Enlightenment, liberal democracy and totalitarianism, freedom and its enemies, and the West and its enemies created a whole new intellectual climate.

But Cold War liberalism's extraordinary influence over Anglo-American politics and culture gave a misleading picture of its inner coherence. Much progress in post-1945 Europe and America was actually achieved through social-welfarist programmes borrowed from socialism. As it happened, the discrediting of socialism in 1989 left liberalism without its most fortifying challenger and interlocutor. Social-welfarism was already being abandoned in Western Europe and America. Liberalism in the 1990s subsided tamely into a shallow economism, the materialistic and mechanistic ideology of neoliberalism. And it is the latter's retro assumption that the real is the rational and that there are no alternatives that has made us incapable of grasping much of today's political phenomena.

Certainly, those who try to explain the irruption of archaisms in the West's postmodern societies, such as identifying and persecuting scapegoats, can no longer rely on the ideological determinisms of the left and the right, not to mention the 'Third Way'. These competing schemes for achieving the good life have underpinned our knowledge of human society and explained historical events through a teleology of progress. Much intellectual work during and after the Cold War has gone into constructing personalities, epochs and cultures as self-contained totalities and awesome models: Winston Churchill, Western Civilization, liberalism and modernity.

The metaphysical big bang of our time threatens not just these vanity projects, the identity politics of elites, but democracy itself. Religion and tradition have been steadily discarded since the late eighteenth century in the hope that rationally self-interested individuals can form a liberal political community which defines its shared laws, ensuring dignity and equal rights for each citizen, irrespective of ethnicity, race, religion and gender. This basic premise of secular modernity, menaced so far by religious fundamentalists, is now endangered by elected demagogues in its very heartlands, Europe and the United States.

Where do we go from here? We can of course continue to define the crisis of democracy through reassuring dualisms: liberalism versus authoritarianism, religion versus secularism, and that sort of thing. It may be more rewarding to think of democracy as a profoundly fraught emotional and social condition, which has now become universally unstable. It will at least allow us to examine the workings of *ressentiment* across the different political regimes and classes today, and to understand why ethno-nationalist supremacism and misogyny grow in tandem with social mobility in India and Turkey as well as stagnation and decline in America and Britain.

The elevation of a rancorous Twitter troll into the world's most powerful man is the latest of many reminders that the idealized claims of Anglo-American elites about democracy and liberalism never actually conformed to the political and economic reality at home. The latter was built originally with the help of racist and imperialist violence; furthermore, it was being constantly transformed, even malformed, in recent decades by globalization and terrorism. In the era of crises that began on 9/11, the thin content of Cold War ideologies mostly evaporated, leaving a residue of nostalgic longing for the certitudes of the anti-totalitarian, 'liberal' West.

Shortly before he died, Tony Judt, the most distinguished of Cold War liberals, hoped that the young would resurrect the social-democratic ideals of his youth by discovering 'the politics of social cohesion based around collective purposes'.[16] In his latest book, France's foremost liberal thinker Pierre Manent gives a highbrow gloss to Michel Houellebecq's puckish advocacy of Islam as a post-Enlightenment creed. And Simon Schama tweeted after Trump's victory that we need a new Churchill to fight fascism in Europe and America.

Such breast-beating or chest-thumping amounts to a truly irrational demand: that the present abolish itself, making way for a return to the past. It tries to avoid the painful fact that the very preconditions for the endeavours of the traditional left and right, which aimed at building solidarity around class, race, gender and nation, have been rapidly disappearing. Lamentations – that we lack the right sort of spine-stiffening leader/rational culture/political community/

religiosity/gender solidarity/nationhood – ignore the fragmented nature of our politics, society and technology, which, ever-mutating, have long been hybrid and indeterminate: as prone to enshrine LGBT rights as to reinstate torture and disseminate fake news. Nor does a longing for the good old days adequately respond to the massive crisis of legitimacy of democratic institutions today.

Political antidotes to the sinister pathologies unleashed by Modi, Erdoğan, Putin, Brexit and Trump require a reckoning with the bad new days – something a lot more forward-looking than models of solidarity inspired by Islam, nationalist pedagogies for the oppressed, or a dauntless faith in globalization eventually delivering the promised goods. This necessary work can only be enabled by a richer, more varied picture of human experience and needs outlined by the masters of suspicion.

Our quantitative obsession with what counts and what can therefore be counted and analysed has for too long excluded what does not count: subjective emotions. For nearly three decades, the religion of technology and GDP and the crude nineteenth-century calculus of self-interest have dominated politics and intellectual life. Today, the society of entrepreneurial individuals ordered around the evidently rational market reveals unplumbed depths of misery and despair; it spawns a nihilistic rebellion against order itself.

With so many of our landmarks in ruins, we can barely see where we are headed, let alone chart a path. But even to get our basic bearings we need, above all, greater precision in matters of the soul. Otherwise we risk resembling, in our infatuation with rational motivations and outcomes, those observers 'in the middle of a rapidly flowing river' who, Tocqueville wrote, 'stare obstinately at some scraps of debris that are still visible on the riverbanks, even as the current is pulling us along and forcing us backward toward the abyss'.[17]

Notes

1 Letter from Sigmund Freud to Frederik van Eeden, 28 December 1914; quoted in Ernest Jones, *The Life and Work of Sigmund*

Freud, Vol. II: *Years of Maturity 1901–1919*, New York: Basic Books, 1955, pp. 368–9.

2 Robert Musil, 'Helpless Europe. A Digressive Journey', in *Precision and Soul: Essays and Addresses*, Chicago and London: University of Chicago Press, 1990, p. 123.

3 Letter from Freud to Eeden, 28 December 1914.

4 Michael Ignatieff, 'Messianic America: Can He Explain It?', *New York Review of Books*, 19 November 2015.

5 Karl Marx, *Capital: A Critique of Political Economy*, Vol. I, Part II, New York: Cosimo, 2007, p. 668, fn. 2.

6 Thomas Piketty, 'We Must Rethink Globalization, or Trumpism Will Prevail', *Guardian*, 16 November 2016, at https://www.theguardian.com/commentisfree/2016/nov/16/globalization-trump-inequality-thomas-piketty (retrieved November 2016).

7 Gary Younge, 'How Trump Took Middle America', *Guardian*, at https://www.theguardian.com/membership/2016/nov/16/how-trump-took-middletown-muncie-election (retrieved November 2016).

8 Mike Davis, 'Not a Revolution – Yet', 15 November 2016, at http://www.versobooks.com/blogs/2948-not-a-revolution-yet (retrieved November 2016).

9 Fyodor Dostoevsky, *Notes From the Underground*, New York: Dover, 1992, p. 14.

10 Musil, 'Helpless Europe', p. 131.

11 Sigmund Freud, *The Future of an Illusion*, London: Penguin, 2004, p. 3.

12 Alexis de Tocqueville, *Democracy in America*, New York: Vintage, 1945, Book II, Chapter I.

13 Alexis de Tocqueville, *Journeys to England and Ireland*, London and New Brunswick: Transaction, 2003, p. 116.

14 Albert Camus, *The Rebel: An Essay on Man in Revolt*, New York: Vintage Books, 1991, p. 17.

15 Stephen Kotkin, *Magnetic Mountain: Stalinism as a Civilization*, Berkeley: University of California Press, 1997, p. 364.

16 Tony Judt (with Timothy Snyder), *Thinking the Twentieth Century*, London: Penguin, 2012, p. 386.

17 Quoted in Leo Damrosch, *Tocqueville's Discovery of America*, New York: Farrar, Straus and Giroux, 2010, p. 91.

10

The courage to be audacious

Robert Misik

It is now almost thirty years since Pierre Bourdieu wrote a little essay with the title 'Penser la politique'. It opens with these sentences:

> We live lives flooded with politics. We swim in the eternal and ever-changing current of the daily prattle about the chances and the merits of interchangeable candidates. We have no need to read the daily or weekly editorials of newspapers and magazines or their 'analyses' ... These political discussions are, like the idle chatter about good or bad weather, essentially ephemeral.[1]

At that time, something was in the wind and we are now confronted with its results, at least in those places that we used to call 'the Western world'. Old ideological parties, which at the same time were also class parties and milieu parties, find that their vitality has drained away over the course of time; the familiar type of party leader has vanished and has been gradually replaced by the new type of professional career politician. All professional politicians together constituted the field of politics and the professional politician's reference system was other professional politicians. In the eyes of the public, they increasingly formed a separate sphere whose members competed for small advantages but who were bound together in a close complicity.

Even worse, it looked to ordinary people as if members of the political establishment were striving to accommodate themselves to the new elite of the global economy. The professional politicians maintained close contact with that elite while its ties to the voters slackened. On top of everything else a new hermetic jargon sprang up that the public simply couldn't stand hearing any longer. And in addition to all that, for the last twenty years the incomes of workers and the lower middle class have stagnated, a fact that has been absorbed into the interpretative scheme of 'them up there, the elite, they couldn't care less, they haven't even noticed'.

This provides us with some of the ingredients that have all coalesced in the Brexit referendum, in Donald Trump's election as US president and, more generally, in the rise of right-wing populism in Europe. What began on the margins and then spread through society as flickerings of discontent has now ended up expanding into potential majorities that threaten to undermine pluralistic democracy. The rise of authoritarian anti-politics, however, is not the cause but the consequence of a failure on the part of established politics, above all the parties of the democratic left, which is why I shall speak primarily about them in what follows.

Let's talk about class

A new era dawned with the world-historical changes we associate with the year 1989. This goes for the progressive parties and the diverse milieus that supported them as well as for new milieus that have come into being since. And what is at issue is not simply the demise of actually existing socialism, the fall of the Wall, the end of the confrontation of hostile blocs or the loss of conviction in 'socialist' narratives. In fact, a variety of processes overlapped in those years. 'The end of history' was proclaimed, as was the triumph of capitalism and of a particular form of pluralistic liberal democracy. Market fundamentalism and neoliberalism became the dominant ideologies. At the same time, Western societies found themselves in the grip of further modernization processes, such as the rise of many young people from the working class into the urban middle class. Working class? Surely there was no longer any such thing! And what was left of it would soon dissolve in the contemporary liquid modernity.

Moreover, socialist and social-democratic parties would themselves become middle-class parties with only a vague idea about the real nature of the people who voted for them. The structural networks in working-class districts that had previously formed the core of the party organizations now dissolved, became porous and felt out of date. In reality, however, our societies were not homogenized into middle-class societies. There were many 'losers', but they were forgotten.

But even that puts the situation too crudely. We are not dealing with crass dichotomies between 'absolute winners' and 'absolute losers'. The group of people who more or less consciously think of themselves as the forgotten men and women is by no means homogeneous.

It consists, first, of the middle class in employment, whose members had never thought of themselves as belonging to the 'working class' and would not be described as such by sociologists (in contrast to the United States, where 'working class' and 'middle class' are often used synonymously and where it seems far more natural to define oneself as 'working class'). Office workers, plumbers, workers with a decent income nevertheless rightly feel threatened by the changes in the global economy. Their wages and salaries have been stagnating for years and they know that they could more easily fall under the wheels in a competitive society than was the case two decades ago. They sense that the ice beneath their feet is getting thinner.

These groups are not identical with those who have to fear immediate economic collapse, nor with those who work hard but earn very little – people like the new service industry proletariat (the shop assistant at the baker's, the parcel deliveryman, etc.). Nor do they have anything in common with people who cannot find any job at all because they lack qualifications. Nor are any of these people identical with 'the poor'; quite the opposite. These sectors of the population are proud of being able to support their families and do not automatically rejoice over welfare programmes that set out to help the poor. The American legal scholar Joan C. Williams has analysed the different threats to and the resulting political and emotional reactions of the 'white working class' in her essay 'What So Many People Don't Get About the U.S. Working Class'.[2] Other things being equal, her map of social situations can be transferred to the majority of European countries.

Nevertheless, some things can be said to apply to the members of all these social groups. They all have the feeling that, politically, there is no longer anyone to speak up on their behalf. They all have the feeling that globalization and European integration generate more costs than benefits for them. And in general terms, they are right. In the current debates about the economy it is still unclear whether more free trade and more deregulation will bring greater benefits or whether the drawbacks have long since gained the upper hand. One thing, however, has ceased to be disputed. Even if trade and deregulation may produce benefits for a nation 'in the aggregate', these benefits are unfairly distributed, which is why there are always winners and losers. And those who are not among the winners know full well after twenty-five years that competition is increasing, social and financial stress is on the rise, and that the formulae contained in the Sunday sermons of the preachers of globalization are nothing but hot air.

All these groups sense that the established progressive parties have generally ceased to be interested in them and that their representatives have themselves joined the global upper class. And again they are not entirely mistaken. To put it differently: our societies are still segregated into classes and we do not even have a clear idea what these persistent class fissures and the new social divisions look like.

Cultural alienation

Progressive parties such as the Austrian Social Democratic Party (SPÖ) have always relied on precarious alliances between different social groupings. With hindsight, we tend to think that these alliances were always harmonious, but the abyss separating, for example, a sophisticated left-wing intellectual such as Max Adler and a folksy trade-union official from Upper Styria was presumably about more than trifling differences in lifestyle even in the 1920s. Working class – that always also meant that the man was the head of the household; the size of income was a measure of masculinity and one did not have much time for intellectual mollycoddling. Even so, the alliance managed to hold together, one way or another. Let's not act like blue-eyed innocents about this. Today, too, in the 'working classes', in the middle class of people with jobs, among the various kinds of office workers, in the new service-industry proletariat, but also among people who have been left behind economically, the operative cultural ideas are quite different from those of the progressive middle classes and the academic milieus in the urban centres.

In the meantime, a further factor has emerged. Traditional milieus have the feeling that the members of urban, cosmopolitan groups look down on them and their lifestyles. Their economic insecurity is compounded by social insecurity; their status is doubly threatened. The Swiss political scientist Silja Häusermann has described this situation in an interview:

> It is neither the poor nor the precariat, but the lower middle classes that are voting for right-wing nationalist parties. These people are not about to become impoverished but they do feel insecure and fear their standard of living may decline. They are laying claim to a status they no longer possess – as employees, as the male breadwinners of the family. They are dissatisfied with the way the world is going. That's all put rather generally, but somehow or other everything is going in a direction that seems wrong to them: for women and young people, in the job market and education ...[3]

People from cultural milieus that they could think of as conventional – and therefore as hegemonic – only a couple of years ago (though they presumably did not think this consciously, but merely took it for granted) now suddenly have the feeling that they are no longer respected. And again, they are not entirely mistaken. No one has given such a blunt, unsparing account of these processes as Didier Eribon in *Returning to Reims*. His parents were communists; he studied in Paris and is forced to admit in retrospect that 'deep inside myself I experienced a rejection of working-class life as I knew it'.[4] Today his family votes for the Front National. Not because they have become racist (they were always racist), but because they feel culturally devalued and no longer feel represented by the existing left-wing parties.

In the meantime, the social change has reached the point where, if they wish for success, left-wing parties must rely on two different milieus or groups of activists and voters of roughly the same size. On the one hand, the modern, left-wing or left-liberal urban middle classes, and on the other, the various segments of the working classes described above. In crude terms, if a left-wing party aims to secure 40 per cent of the vote in an election, voters from each of these backgrounds will contribute roughly half of the necessary total. But there are dramatic differences between the two groups.

A few weeks after the Brexit vote, John Harris wrote an article in the *Guardian* entitled 'Does the Left Have a Future?,'[5] offering a detailed analysis of the dilemmas facing the Labour Party. In it he argues convincingly that the problems facing left-wing parties cannot be readily solved overnight with a simple policy change. To exaggerate only slightly, we could say that the Blairites turned Labour into a middle-class social-democratic party, which sought to accommodate the attitudes of the urban middle class while ignoring the working class completely. So now the party shifts to the left and elects Jeremy Corbyn as leader in order to regain the trust of ordinary people.

But matters are not so straightforward. Corbyn himself is the hero of progressive students, internationalists and convinced leftists. Such groups want a programme that is very different from that of the working-class voters who voted for Brexit, of people who believe that immigrants are taking their jobs and that left-wing academics are far too concerned with LGBT rights and questions of political correctness. So a move to the left will not automatically lead to the creation of a successful progressive block consisting of these two large groupings. Even worse, a move to the left might result in Corbyn losing the support of people from progressive urban backgrounds without gaining significantly more support from the working class.

The one group of supporters is opposed to immigration and multiculturalism, the other is in favour of internationalism, human rights and solidarity. The former wants protectionism, the latter undoubtedly profits from globalization.

The one group voted for Brexit by an overwhelming margin, the other voted against Brexit by a no less overwhelming majority. In other words, there is not only a deep divide between the two – the gulf between them looks as if it can hardly be bridged.

Restoring momentum to the European Union

Forging a new alliance between these different groups is not going to be a walk in the park. Clear-cut ideas are a necessary precondition for that alliance, though by no means a sufficient one. In any event, a political change of course is needed.

The dominance of neoliberal ideas will have to be driven back at many different levels. To begin with, at the level of political and economic discourse. Here at least, there has been some progress since the financial crisis. Fifteen years ago the hegemony of market radicalism was unquestioned; the mantra of increased flexibility, globalization, deregulation, structural reform and competitiveness went basically unchallenged. The majority of traditional, reformist centre-left parties adapted themselves to the dominant paradigm, and consequently no longer had any paradigm or ideas of their own that they could have confidence in. They mistrusted their own ideas and so capitulated to those of their opponents.

Now the picture has changed. The fact that across the board austerity doesn't work has now become obvious to even the most pig-headed believer (with the exception perhaps of Wolfgang Schäuble and a few well-paid lobbyists who exemplify Upton Sinclair's assertion that 'it is difficult to get a man to understand something, when his salary depends upon his not understanding it!'). Scarcely anyone who wishes to be taken halfway seriously will now dispute the fact that growth cannot be generated by reducing incomes throughout the Eurozone. The mantra of competitiveness, which leads only to a race to the bottom, has brought the pluralist societies to the verge of collapse.

Economists from Paul Krugman to Joseph Stiglitz and Branko Milanović, from Dani Rodrik via Thomas Piketty to Mariana Mazzucato, have not only attacked the prevailing paradigm in countless articles and books, but have also developed a programme for contemporary progressives. It involves emphasizing the role of the state and the importance of a fairer income distribution as well as the growth-inhibiting effects of an excess of international competition. In the meantime, in the global debate – from magazines close to Wall Street, such as *Forbes*, to the much-read website vox.com – there is even talk of a 'New Liberal Consensus'. Of course, that does not mean that there is something like a progressive hegemony in economic debates, but we can say that the dominance of the neoliberal programme has given way to a 'balance of terror'. Perhaps we may also venture the assertion that the neoliberal view of things will soon have lost its influence almost entirely. In the political battles that are approaching, left-liberal programmes will confront those of populist nationalists – a duel in which the assumptions of the old neoliberal elites will perish. (The traditional centre-right parties, which are usually flexible, will attempt to adopt one of two positions. They will either present themselves as parties of social justice or, following the example of the Bavarian CSU, copy the right-wing populists on specific issues or imitate them to the point where they are more or less indistinguishable, as is the case with a broad section of US Republicans.)

So the problem is no longer an absence of progressive ideas. It is rather how we are to translate these ideas into political practice. This applies in a quite particular way to the European Union. The political and economic architecture of the Union is implicitly neoliberal in the sense that it makes the practical implementation of left-wing ideas extraordinarily difficult. The EU consists of twenty-eight member states (for the time being), the Eurozone of nineteen. Even slight changes of course presuppose a consensus among the governments (or at least a majority), and even then any change would be diluted in the system of multi-level governance of the EU Parliament and the EU Commission. If one member state elects a left-wing government it will soon be confronted by the narrow limits of what is politically doable, brutally so as in the case of the Syriza government in Greece, or somewhat more gently as in the case of the left-wing government in Portugal.

Considered systematically, three things are needed for a real change of course. First, vibrant national parties of the left with enough credibility to win elections in their own country. Second, an expansion of the hegemony of progressive discourse in Europe so as to create the conditions for change. And third, alliances between revived left-wing governments at European level. None of this is easy, but nor is it impossible.

Looking at the situation empirically, what we have in Europe today are traditional social democrats who over recent decades have adopted the neoliberal paradigm to a greater or lesser degree and who are now engaged with greater or lesser success in reinventing themselves. The spectrum extends from German social democracy via the badly bruised French Socialist Party, the Swedish Social Democratic Party, which has been in power in a highly successful alliance with the Greens, the Austrian SPÖ under the leadership of an energetic young chancellor, right down to the UK opposition Labour Party with Jeremy Corbyn at its head. At the same time, new parties of the left have come into being which, like Syriza, are replacing the established social-democratic parties, or are in competition with them, as is the case with Podemos (which has ended up damaging both parties) or with the Portuguese left-wing parties that have formed an alliance with the governing socialists.

A clear view of reality

The progressive parties must work to become credible representatives of the economically most vulnerable parts of society once again. For that to succeed a number of points have to be heeded:

First, we must finally acknowledge the reality described above.

Second, after thirty years in which ordinary people have paid the price for neoliberal globalization and are full of frustrations, it will be fatal if left-wing parties are perceived as part of the Establishment. They need a programme and a language of radical change and they must be seen to seek a confrontation with the globalized elites rather than a compromise with them.

Third, everything that can be seen (even if mistakenly) as arrogance towards the voters must go. Christian Kern, the new chairman of the Social Democratic Party of Austria, made an important point in his inaugural speech at the party conference in June 2016:

> I believe that as our very first step we must do one thing: we must eliminate from our vocabulary the sentence 'We have to reach out to the people.' Of course, this is not meant to sound patronising, but that's how it may well come across. And it is also both absurd and mistaken because what does it mean 'reach out to the people'? We are the people! We are the people and we belong to these people and these people belong to us.

Fourth, this does not by a long chalk mean that we need to endorse the prejudices that are undoubtedly present in the working class. Moreover, it is by no means true that these sectors of the population are furious because the 'cultural left' is calling for a third toilet for transgender persons. They are furious because they have the feeling that such demands are getting *lots* of attention, while their own economic and social situation is not being given *any attention at all*.

Fifth, good jobs, rising incomes, affordable housing, education and life opportunities for their children, and similar subjects are the key issues. All those who fail to show convincingly that this is what concerns them, or who cannot demonstrate that they at least have a plausible plan (even if it is a plan that can only be implemented with great patience and step by step), are doomed to failure.

Sixth, as the networks of the workers' movement that structured the lifeworlds of underprivileged districts have declined, black holes have appeared, which is why people still living there feel abandoned. For this reason, it is important to build modern structures at urban district level, following, for example, the models created by Community Organizing. In short, it is crucial to make oneself useful to one's fellow citizens, to make sure that groups of the most diverse kind are empowered to organize themselves, articulate their own interests and translate them into practice.

Seventh, don't make the mistake of dismissing the working class as misogynistic, anti-feminist and xenophobic. Even the worst macho steelworker living in the age of the one-child family wants his daughter to have every opportunity for advancement and to get a good, decently paid job.

Eighth, activists should be encouraged and trained to become party officials who will have credibility in these environments. Left-wing parties today are represented chiefly by people from the educated middle class, while in working-class suburbs there are far too many apparatchiks of the type prominent in the 1970s, who believe they have the ear of the people while the latter would far rather throw them right out of the pub with a good kick up the backside. In dead party organizations it is only such apparatchiks who rise to the top. That is why we need channels that enable good, young people from among middle-class workers and the working class to succeed.

Dilemmas that will remain

Left-wing intellectuals of whatever stripe sometimes have the unpleasant habit of acting as if all the problems of the world could be solved overnight if only people would heed their advice. This superior posturing (and I too have not always been completely immune to it) normally stands in stark contrast to their chronic lack of success. If matters were really so simple, each and every one of us would have long since founded a new party and in a trice led it to an absolute majority. If we were to take the eight points outlined above as a guide, something would presumably be achieved, but it would not resolve every problem. A number of dilemmas would still remain.

The rampant discontent has a variety of causes. In fact, we are really talking about two sorts of discontent. On the one hand, the resentment felt by middle-class progressives towards the outmoded apparatchik-parties and the self-inflicted decoupling of politics as an end itself. On the other hand, the dissatisfaction of the economically most vulnerable social groups who feel that no one is interested in their plight, even as things keep getting worse. New, left-wing alliances – reorganized parties, newly founded parties, movements, etc. – will only be able to translate this humus, in which right-wing populism is thriving so vigorously, into the yeast of progressive politics if they possess a forward-looking message. A rhetoric of 'defence' ('We are defending the welfare state!', for example) or even the dogged 'keep it up!' is doomed to failure unless we can at the same time offer a vision that keeps people's hopes alive. Anyone who comes forward with the implicit promise 'Vote for us because we shall make sure that things will only get worse slowly!' may just as well hand over the keys of office to the leader of the nearest right-wing populist party. What we need, finally, is what Barack Obama has called 'the audacity of hope'.[6]

Of course, it is not easy to renew the old progressive alliance between those who want to fight for new civil liberties and modernize our societies and those who want to stand up for economic welfare (in short, the alliance between what used to be called 'the bourgeois intellectuals and the working class'). Some even think that this is no longer possible: John Harris for example, but also Silja Häusermann, who claims that 'whatever the left does, it will lose votes from the one side or the other'. But just because something is not easy doesn't mean that it is impossible. Earlier progressive movements, from the workers' movements of the nineteenth century to the American Civil Rights movement, did not come into being in situations in which conditions were straightforward and victory easily won. On the contrary, the left was not established so as to have things easy but in order to bring about the impossible. It was created to improve the world and the condition of human beings in the teeth of adversity and apparent hopelessness, to fight for human rights and liberty and to flood the societies of the world with democracy.

Translated by Rodney Livingstone

Notes

1 Pierre Bourdieu, 'Penser la politique', *Actes de la recherche en sciences sociales*, 71–2 (1988), pp. 2–3.
2 Joan C. Williams, 'What So Many People Don't Get About the American Working Class', *Harvard Business Review*, 10 November 2016, at www.hbr.org/2016/11/what-so-many-people-dont-get-about-the-u-s-working-class (retrieved December 2016).

3 Carlos Hanimann, ' "Egal was die Linke macht" ', interview with Silja Häusermann, *Die Wochenzeitung*, 24 November 2016, at www.woz.ch/-74ce (retrieved December 2016).
4 Didier Eribon, *Returning to Reims*, introduced by George Chauncey, translated by Michael Lucey, Cambridge, MA: MIT Press, 2013, p. 30.
5 John Harris, 'Does the Left Have a Future?', *Guardian*, 6 September 2016, at www.theguardian.com/politics/2016/sep/06/does-the-left-have-a-future (retrieved December 2016).
6 Barack Obama, *The Audacity of Hope: Thoughts on Reclaiming the American Dream*, New York: Crown, 2006. The book title refers to a formulation in a speech by Obama at the Democratic National Convention in July 2004 at which John Kerry was nominated presidential candidate.

11

Decivilization: on regressive tendencies in Western societies

Oliver Nachtwey

It wouldn't have taken much for the first black US president to have been succeeded by the first woman president. Instead, the office is now occupied by a misogynistic, xenophobic and paranoid property developer who is scarcely able to control his affects and who may not even wish to do so. In many respects Donald Trump embodies in his person the negation of everything the West claims to be: societies with self-control in which the forces of social progress are at home, which drive Enlightenment, equal rights and social integration forward. However, something in these societies has started to slip; their self-image has taken a knock. A kind of uncontrolled rage has entered the political public sphere; hatred is openly expressed; dangerous feelings, fantasies of violence and even the wish to kill are frivolously voiced.

People's affect control has been eroded in many ways: on the internet, in the street and in everyday behaviour. Norbert Elias has described the process of civilization as a long-term trend of social interaction leading to greater control of our feelings and the ability to organize our lives. But if we put all the symptoms mentioned above together we have the dangerous prospect of a regressive process of decivilization.

The echo chambers and filter bubbles of the internet undoubtedly reinforce feelings of resentment. But it would be misleading to think of what are – literally – social media as the cause of resentment, rather than as simply the force that gives it shape. To blame the algorithms would be like holding the radio responsible for Goebbels. And we should not forget that social media had previously been regarded as the source of democratic aspirations (as in the context of the Arab Spring, for example). Our task, therefore, is to analyse the social causes of decivilization.

The basic constellation that has brought about this social, cultural and political 'malaise, this discontent',[1] is marked by major non-simultaneities in the way people lead their lives, and in the realm of equal rights and inequality. Two examples from the US: the life expectancy of Americans in general has risen, while that of white American workers has fallen.[2] Black Americans have made great strides in participating in social, cultural and political institutions; it is a long time since they were made to sit in separate compartments in the Southern states. The years of formal segregation are over – so long as we don't look too closely. If we do, however, we see that liberal equality goes hand in hand with the mass incarceration of blacks and the creation of a stigmatized lower class.[3]

These problems cannot all be addressed comprehensively in the sketch that follows. However, I should like to develop a few sociological and historical arguments that may conceivably lead to an understanding of the earthquakes that are currently shaking Western industrial societies – and not them alone. Paradoxically, the somewhat reactionary tendencies we are witnessing at present may be seen as a side-effect of social progress. In the case of such non-simultaneous and conflicted developments, in which progress contains retrograde steps within itself, we are looking at the processes of a 'regressive modernization' which characterizes Western capitalist countries today. This frequently applies to the horizontal equality of groups with differing characteristics (sexual or ethnic, for example) that coincides with new vertical inequalities and discriminations.[4] This specific combination of progress and regress has produced normative demands on civilization as well as supposed losers who seek refuge in the regressive affects of decivilization.

Civilization and decivilization

One of the principal theories to seek to explain the civilizing process comes from Norbert Elias. For Elias, civilization is the product of a thoroughgoing transformation of social and personality structures characterized by social differentiation and comprehensive human relationships. This leads to stronger individual self-control, to a new psychic habitus in the control of affect, to a broadening of our thinking processes, and especially to our deferring the immediate gratification of needs as well as a new habit of long-term thinking.[5]

The starting point of the civilizing process lies in the development of central powers and of competition and class distinctions in feudal society. But it is also the result of the rise of particular social groups later on. Between the eighteenth and twentieth centuries, when middle-class strata caught up (and partly merged) with the nobility as well as the higher bourgeoisie and forced the establishment to share their power with them, its members at first championed above all the idea of progress. In addition, they stood for an optimistic view of the future,[6] and from time to time even drew sections of the working class along with them. Because of this upwards movement, in which certain groups shed some of their privileges but in which all groups were swept along by the tide of social modernization, some habitual group conflicts faded into the background.[7]

Elias's civilization theory shared its initial assumptions with Theodor W. Adorno and Max Horkheimer's *Dialectic of Enlightenment*.[8] Both go back to an assumption voiced by Sigmund Freud, according to whom the development of culture is accompanied by the sublimation of the drives, so that at the individual level external constraints are transformed into self-imposed constraints. Adorno and Horkheimer proceed from the premise that a rationalized world is also a world of anonymous domination.

Whereas Adorno and Horkheimer see a tendency towards the total domination of the individual by society, Elias analyses the process of individualization as a transformation of the personality structure that depends historically upon the social balance of power at any one time. However, Elias does not regard the civilizing process as either continuous or as organically progressive; civilization in his view is 'never completed and always endangered'.[9] That is why it is constantly threatened by its opposite: decivilization. Adorno and Horkheimer, too, thought of decivilization as an immanent risk of modernization. 'Instead of entering a truly human state', they wrote, humanity may be 'sinking into a new kind of barbarism'.[10]

In this essay I shall follow up both tracks of the decivilizing process. In so doing, I take the view that we should combine the position of Critical Theory, which emphasizes the importance of systemic constraints on the individual, with that of Elias, who explains the process of individualization together with the importance of the changing balance of power in society. A combination of these two points of view can contribute to our understanding of the current decivilizing processes – if we add a further dimension, namely the role of community and intermediary associations. I shall first develop a diagnosis of the effects of (neo)liberal systemic constraints on the individual and of other drivers of disintegration in the context of regressive modernization. Secondly, I shall discuss the role of groups or individuals who experience social and economic decline, before bringing the two strands of the argument together with a view to shedding light on the processes of decivilization.

Individualization and regressive modernization

Individualization was originally an element of the civilizing process. The fact that its members can act as autonomous subjects belongs to the basic self-description of a modern society. The process of individualization is based on emancipation from traditional restrictive social forms: traditional social relationships, families, local communities, neighbourhoods – these have all reduced in significance. The paradox, however, is that in having shaken off such traditional social ties, the individual has in the last analysis become more socially dependent than ever.[11] For example, as more and more people develop mobile lifestyles, they frequently no longer live close to their parents and so need a nursery where their children can be looked after. But because of the de-collectivization of

the welfare state and the dismantling of its reserves of solidarity, the individual is increasingly becoming individualized
in a negative way. The risk of decline that has become the
hallmark of Western capitalisms is no longer counteracted.

In this context it is easy to overlook the role of communities and intermediary associations. However static and
stuffy the traditional lifeworlds and (class) backgrounds may
have been, they were spaces for counter-interpretations that
provided relief. One example is unemployment, where social
risks were viewed not as the result of individual failure but
as a shared destiny. Associations and clubs, places that we
would regard today as part of civil society, not only provided
refuge and relief from social pressures but were places in
which society – even a counter-culture – might be organized,
albeit on a small scale. This applied both to the working
class and to the more middle-class strata. People had a sense
of agency and a place where their own voices counted. They
could articulate grievances but also discover a form of socialization, collective identity, social integration and hence also
social control. In this sense communities and intermediary
associations are always also schools of democracy and civil-
ity.[12] The waning importance of community and intermediary associations means that the individual, faced with social
pressures and change, is frequently forced to rely entirely on
his own resources.

In this sense the dystopian perspective adopted by Adorno
and Horkheimer in regard to individualization seems to have
been confirmed in certain respects. After the financial crisis
a variety of commentators did indeed proclaim the end of
neoliberalism, and in fact the state has re-entered the realm of
economic policy. In the event, however, neoliberalism was not
buried but merely secured. The market remains the reference
point for all aspects of life. Pierre Bourdieu has called such
mechanisms *symbolic violence*.[13] We have now internalized
the market and regard it as self-evident; we assent to its logic,
partly willingly, partly against our will. In neoliberalism the
burden of self-restraint, of permanent sublimation, is great.
We have always to be happy to compete, to compare, to
measure ourselves against others and to optimize. Unreason-
able demands, setbacks, humiliations and failures have to
be chalked up to oneself – and we then just have to wait

cheerfully for new opportunities. In general, in view of the corresponding cultural changes, it is traditionalists who feel most uncertain about which standards of behaviour should apply. And anyone wishing to oppose neoliberalism will find themselves *punished* by the market and the state in a harmonious alliance. The Greeks have a story to tell about that.

Neoliberalism, with its quasi-religious belief in the market, is a contemporary instance of 'instrumental reason'.[14] According to Horkheimer, within the framework of the rule of instrumental reason everything is subject to a means-ends rationality, the logic of mastery over nature and oneself. The profoundly authoritarian belief in the market is 'an anonymous god who enslaves men' because it thinks that there is no alternative to itself.[15] Horkheimer's interpretation turns out to be hugely productive in enabling us to understand the transformation of autonomy into authoritarianism. The absence of alternatives to the market compels the individual to internalize it. For the champions of the Enlightenment the conviction that the individual can master the world was an article of faith. Under the aegis of a total instrumentalized reason, the individual's mastery of the world turns into the world's total control of the individual. Market-conforming individuality now becomes society's imperative.

The modern individual's naturally acquired autonomy is now tied to his market performance. The winners receive an autonomy dividend; the losers are disciplined and stigmatized. The modern individual is as dependent on institutions as he ever was, but he is now increasingly desocialized. He is being changed from a citizen integrated in a more or less organized community with institutions of collective solidarity into a market citizen, a customer with rights. However, such disembedded markets produce permanent uncertainty and cause the erosion of many individuals' sense of agency – they no longer believe that they can master current situations, let alone the future. Their need for transparency, control and safety is no longer satisfied. And even our permissive culture has paradoxically led to an increase in feelings of guilt, since although we are now permitted to do all sorts of things, we must remain civilized and economically productive. In short, self-restraint and internalization become just another form of social coercion – emotions pile up, civilized self-control flags, and resentments are released as through a safety valve.

Processes of social disintegration also play a part. For example, following Talcott Parsons, Axel Honneth has argued that (a) the legal system, (b) the economy and (c) the family all have a dual function, that of systemic and social integration. To be sure, in recent decades the workings of these subsystems have changed: they have become sources of disintegration and have even led to a 'barbarisation of social conflict'.[16] We can discern a kind of regressive modernization in each of these spheres. (a) There has been some advance in establishing equal rights for minorities in recent times, but whereas great strides have been made in regard to the equality of the sexes, ethnic minorities and LGBTs, etc., *social* rights (of contract workers, for example) have become fragmented. This has led (b) to an increase in precarious working conditions in the economy. Looked at from this perspective, the emancipation processes of the last thirty years have followed the logic of liberalism, which has yoked together cultural equality and a deregulated market. Honneth emphasizes, lastly, that, according to Parsons, (c) the role of the father as head of the household contributed to social pacification. Through this role, it was possible to compensate for failures to achieve recognition at work. In the meantime, however, many men have lost not only their monopoly as breadwinners, but also their symbolic role as head of the family.

Decline and the erosion of civilization

The advances in the standards of civilized behaviour in the twentieth century were based not just on increasing self-control but also on 'maintenance of the accustomed standard of living'.[17] The central prerequisites, then, include a high degree of social and psychological security. Struggles around status and rank still existed in societies that were more and more integrated and egalitarian, but they were increasingly displaced into spheres such as sport, consumption and culture.

Moreover, from the middle of the twentieth century onwards new social movements arose, which shifted the balance of power in society. We need think only of the women's movement and movements whose supporters demanded recognition of their subjective rights and their sexual, etc., identities. The established classes maintained their positions but in the latter part of the century new insecurities with regard to status, identity and conduct emerged.

Nevertheless, since the 1980s and, at the latest, the '90s, the basic dynamics of Western societies have fundamentally changed. The course of collective progress has come to a halt; not everyone is upwardly mobile and some find themselves on the way down – especially such groups as skilled workers from the lower middle class, who had previously thought of themselves as established. Of course, social progress had always created losers, but today's losers are frequently the semi-established classes of former times.

Elias had two dimensions in mind: first, the rise and fall of groups within a state; second, the position of countries in the global system. Looking at past developments, he concluded: 'The immediate effects of ... decline, of a loss of power and status, are usually feelings of despondency and disillusionment. Feelings of worthlessness and aimlessness interspersed with tendencies towards cynicism, nihilism and withdrawal into oneself can gain the upper hand.'[18] More particularly, at the level of the global system, specific groups in what used to be the leading Western nations have shown a relative decline over the last twenty or thirty years. And it is often these very groups that are particularly susceptible to authoritarian programmes along the lines of 'Let's Make X Great Again'. This has a lot to do with the global development of capitalism, which is experiencing its own specific form of regressive modernization.

We can begin by noting that developments in the economy globally have been extraordinarily positive. Income inequality between nations has been falling since the late 1980s, a fact related to the growth in the Asian economies. The BRICS nations (Brazil, Russia, India, China and South Africa) have caught up and left behind their status as 'developing countries'. It is in these countries that the globalization winners live, the new global middle classes, even if they are still relatively poor when compared to the middle-class living standards of Western nations. In the Western world, however, inequality is on the rise because lower and middle incomes have stagnated or at best grown only minimally.[19] The middle and working classes of the old industrialized world are the losers from global modernization. They are forced to look on as they lose ground to three different groups: the cosmopolitan elites, the highly qualified globalization winners, and the middle classes of the up-and-coming capitalist countries. This is especially so for men with no or few qualifications, who endure additional experiences of decline and insecurity. As we have already indicated, they have frequently lost their status as head of the household and in addition have the feeling that they are being discriminated against in favour of asylum seekers and other minorities. The corresponding resentments do not just arise in moral backwaters, to be seized upon by political opportunists. They are also stoked and legitimized by established players. For example, the Bavarian minister president Horst Seehofer said as long ago as March 2011, 'We shall defend ourselves against immigration into German welfare systems – to the last bullet.' In the light of such comments we need not be astonished at the rhetoric of Pegida.

The decivilizing processes

As reasons for a possible decivilization, Elias refers to power struggles and changes in the relationships between well-established groups and outsiders. 'Such cases of losses of power by former establishments in relation to rising outsider groups triggered bitter resistance, a scarcely realistic longing for the restoration of the old order and not merely for economic reasons.' The groups affected 'feel themselves lowered in their own self-esteem'.[20] Where established segments of the population had the impression that they were threatened by the arrival of outsiders, they reacted with derogatory stigmatizations.[21] Here we find the deeper cause of the decivilizing process. Frequently, for people made insecure under such circumstances,

> no means is too rough or barbaric, because their power and their image of themselves as a great and splendid formation

has a higher value for them than their lives. And the weaker, the more insecure and desperate they become on the road to their decline, the more they develop the sense that they are fighting for their supremacy with their backs against the wall, the more savage for the most part does their behaviour become and the more acute the danger that they will disregard and destroy the civilised standards of conduct on which they pride themselves. That is because, whatever other functions they may serve, civilised standards of conduct are often only meaningful for ruling groups as long as they remain symbols and instruments of their power. As a result, power elites, ruling classes or nations often fight in the name of their superior value, their superior civilisation, with means which are diametrically opposed to the values for which they claim to stand. With their backs against the wall, the champions easily become the greatest destroyers of civilisation. They tend easily to become barbarians.[22]

Such decivilization phenomena make their appearance not just in the lower middle classes but also among the elites. Particularly affected seem to be middle-aged men with average qualifications and an average income. More cannot be said on the subject at present; research is still in its infancy. What do such men have in common, other than that they follow hate messages on the internet or even disseminate them themselves, once they have finished having dinner with their family? They feel devalued and exploited – by the elites, by globalization, by women and by immigrants. They have the impression that they have been turned into social outsiders, a minority in their own country that no one listens to and in whom no one has any interest. They attempt to compensate for this palpable loss of status by the 'negative classification of other groups'.[23] Material and status anxieties are the drivers of resentment, negative emotions, the closing-up of identity and belief in conspiracy theories – features that were recognized early on as characteristics of authoritarian personality structures.[24] Against this background it may be the case that it is the capitulation to the supposed absence of economic alternatives to the market that sets free 'authoritarian aggressions'.[25]

Those who feel socially excluded lose their sense of agency. Many therefore have recourse to specific strategies to restore their self-esteem. These strategies can work in practice or else at the level of perception. A paradoxical result is that such people may seek relief in accepting the coercion of an authoritarian leader. As Elias wrote in connection with National Socialism, uncertain times can lead to 'the longing for external control by a strong ruler'.[26] Resentments enable insecure people to regain self-control, an identity, a new sense of belonging. The basic problem that emerges from the radical process of individualization, Elias maintained, is that of the role of collective identities. After all, people are always dependent on their sense of belonging.[27] Identity politics, then, is also a reaction to the erosion of community and intermediary institutions. Radicalism allows people to feel that they are sovereign beings once again.

Evidently there are a number of groups at present who no longer feel it is worth their while to behave in a civilized manner. As disengaged individuals who are scarcely subject any longer to social control, above all on the internet, and who don't have to take responsibility for their anonymous hate messages, they can give their prejudices free rein. They end up joining emotional coalitions of the resentful – in the Alternative für Deutschland, or on the platforms of Donald Trump or Marine Le Pen. What unites these groups is the negation of civilization in practice in the name of an imagined Western civilization.

Translated by Rodney Livingstone

Notes

1 Leo Löwenthal, *Falsche Propheten. Studien zum Autoritarismus, Schriften*, Vol. 3, Frankfurt am Main: Suhrkamp, 1990 [1949], p. 29.
2 Göran Therborn, 'An Age of Progress?', *New Left Review*, II:99 (2016), p. 35.
3 See Michelle Alexander, *The New Jim Crow: Mass Incarceration in the Age of Colorblindness*, New York: New Press, 2010.
4 See Oliver Nachtwey, *Die Abstiegsgesellschaft. Über das Aufbegehren in der regressiven Moderne*, Berlin: Suhrkamp, 2016 (English translation forthcoming).

5 Norbert Elias, *The Civilizing Process*, Vol. 1, *The History of Manners*; Vol. 2, *State Formation and Civilization*, Oxford: Basil Blackwell, 1978, 1982, both volumes translated by Edmund Jephcott.

6 Later on this resulted in a conservative strand: when the rise of the middle stratum of the bourgeoisie had reached its zenith, its optimism vanished and thereafter it strove increasingly to defend the position it had reached. Its gaze turned less towards the future, and more towards the past and the nation. See Norbert Elias, *The Germans: Power Struggles and the Development of Habitus in the Nineteenth and Twentieth Centuries*, translated by Eric Dunning and Stephen Mennell, Cambridge: Polity, 1997, pp. 134–5.

7 Elias was less interested in class conflicts, since he was chiefly concerned with the long-term transformation of personality structures.

8 Theodor W. Adorno and Max Horkheimer, *Dialectic of Enlightenment*, translated by Edmund Jephcott, Stanford: Stanford University Press, 2002.

9 Elias, *The Germans*, p. 173.

10 Horkheimer and Adorno, *Dialectic of Enlightenment*, p. xiv.

11 See Ulrich Beck, *The Risk Society*, translated by Mark Ritter, London: Sage Publications, 1992.

12 On the decline of civic organization in the United States, see, for example, Robert Putnam, *Bowling Alone: The Collapse and Revival of American Community*, New York: Simon & Schuster, 2000.

13 See, for example, Pierre Bourdieu, *Counterfire: Against the Tyranny of the Market*, London and New York: Verso Books, 2003.

14 See Max Horkheimer, *Critique of Instrumental Reason: Lectures and Essays Since the End of World War II*, translated by Matthew J. O'Connell and others, New York: Continuum, 1974.

15 Max Horkheimer, 'Authority and the Family', in *Critical Theory: Selected Essays*, translated by Matthew J. O'Connell and others, New York: Continuum, 2002, p. 82.

16 Axel Honneth, 'Verwilderung des sozialen Konflikts. Anerkennungskämpfe zu Beginn des 21. Jahrhunderts', in Ophelia Axel, Stephan Lindemann et al. (eds), *Strukturwandel der Anerkennung. Paradoxien sozialer Integration in der Gegenwart*, Frankfurt am Main: Campus, 2013 [2011], pp. 17–39.

17 Elias, *The Germans*, p. 173. These standards also underwent barbaric reverses, above all in the age of fascism.

18 Ibid., p. 359.

19 See Branko Milanović, *Global Inequality: A New Approach For the Age of Globalization*, Cambridge, MA: Harvard University Press, 2016.

20 Elias, *The Germans*, p. 184.

21 Norbert Elias and John L. Scotson, *The Established and the Outsiders*, ed. Cas Wouters, Dublin: UCD Press, 2008 [1965].

22 Elias, *The Germans*, pp. 358–9.

23 Sighard Neckel and Ferdinand Sutterlüty, 'Negative Klassifikationen. Konflikte und die symbolische Ordnung sozialer Ungleichheit', in Wilhelm Heitmeyer and Peter Imbusch (eds), *Integrationspotenziale einer modernen Gesellschaft. Analysen zu gesellschaftlicher Integration und Desintegration*, Wiesbaden: VS, 2005, pp. 409–28.

24 Theodor W. Adorno et al., *The Authoritarian Personality*, New York, Evanston and London: Harper & Row, 1950.

25 See Oliver Decker, Johannes Kiess and Elmar Brähler, *Die stabilisierte Mitte. Rechtsextreme Einstellung in Deutschland 2014*, Leipzig: Kompetenzzentrum für Rechtsextremismus- und Demokratieforschung der Universität Leipzig, 2014, at http://www.research.uni-leipzig.de/kredo/Mitte_Leipzig_Internet.pdf (retrieved December 2016).

26 Elias, *The Germans*, p. 319.

27 Norbert Elias, *The Society of Individuals*, ed. Michael Schröter, translated by Edmund Jephcott, New York and London: Continuum, 2001 [1991].

12

From global regression to post-capitalist counter-movements

César Rendueles

Since 2008, the hegemony that had enabled Western elites to define the limits of political legitimacy for thirty years – setting the boundaries of what we collectively considered possible, impossible, desirable or necessary – has splintered. The crisis has changed the perception of contemporary capitalism's functioning among social groups that used to believe that their interests and those of the global elites overlapped. Today, in contrast, many of these people are well aware that the possibility of a collapsing life – of what Robert Castel calls 'disaffiliation'[1] – has been democratized and is no longer the preserve of migrants, former industrial workers, low-qualified casual workers and other losers from the first phase of neoliberal globalization. It is precisely the different ways of interpreting the nature of this common destiny – whether as a zero-sum game confronting the different victims of the crisis, or as the combined effect of global tendencies – that provide some of the keys for understanding the political, social and cultural convulsions of our time.

As against this, it is significant that the dominant readings of the present historical cycle have a marked economistic slant, as shown by the generalized use of the expression 'the great recession'. To describe what has happened since 2008 – from the Arab Spring to the victory of Syriza, followed by the refugee crisis and Brexit – with a very technical concept that macroeconomics textbooks define as 'at least two consecutive quarters of falling GDP', seems like a bad joke. Besides, the economistic interpretation of the crisis is also ethnocentric and classist. The idea that something exceptional happened in 2008 must seem strange to the hundreds of millions of people for whom financial shocks and the delegitimizing of democratic institutions have been their daily experience for decades. Mexicans and Colombians under forty have literally known nothing other than economic crisis and political decomposition. And something similar is happening to broad sectors in the rich countries.

Sometimes I do a little experiment with my sociology students. I first explain to them the risk figures for relative poverty in Spain, which in 2016 affected something over 22 per cent of the population. I go on to ask them what they imagine this percentage was before the start of the crisis, at the peak of the Spanish economic miracle, when Spain was the eighth-largest world economy. Almost all of them suggest a figure well below 10 per cent. The real situation is that in 2007, 19.7 per cent of Spanish households were already at risk of relative poverty: inequality is not a consequence of the recession but its cause.

In fact, crisis is the historical norm of global turbo-capitalism. First of all because financial catastrophes have followed one another almost without interruption since the early 1980s, affecting, among other countries, Mexico, the United States, Japan, Finland, Thailand, Indonesia, the Philippines, Spain, Russia, Argentina and Iceland. Above all, however, as David Harvey has indicated, because these regional crises have not challenged the neoliberal project but actually reinforced it.[2] The financial collapses caused by deregulation and transnational economic interdependence have been used to drive political reforms designed to reduce workers' negotiating power still further. The same thing has happened with social discontent arising from commercialization: from the early 1980s, neoliberals developed aggressive strategies to manage mental suffering, the degradation of public institutions, increased social fragility, cultural deterioration and political polarization in such a way that they feedback positively on its project.

The contemporary great regression is not so much the start of a new economic era as a result of the strategy that

Western elites adopted in order to overcome the crisis of capital accumulation of the 1970s: a return to globalized 'Manchester school' capitalism that culminated in a crushing victory of the dominant classes. And in a social system such as capitalism – self-expanding and essentially incompatible with any kind of limitation – a crushing victory is always the antechamber to catastrophe.

Emerging counter-movements

In the 1940s, in a similar fashion, Karl Polanyi interpreted the great economic, political, social and intellectual crisis of his time not as an unpredictable anomaly, but as the rational outcome of processes of generalized commercialization that, after sweeping Europe, expanded across the whole world in the colonial whirlwind of the late nineteenth century.[3] From this point of view, the two world wars and the rise of totalitarianism arose from the hidden tensions that had accumulated throughout a long century of *pax mercatoria* and unprecedented economic growth.

Polanyi did not question the legitimacy or the justice of economic liberalism so much as its very possibility. The ideal of the self-regulating market was a utopian and self-destructive project, materially incompatible with any variety of human social life. The free market never has existed and never can exist. Commercialization processes have always required aggressive intervention on the part of the state, in order to mitigate their systemic faults and to break people's resistance to being swept away by the economic hurricane.

The historical option that actually faces us, according to Polanyi, is not one between free market and collective intervention. We can only choose between different types of political mediations, 'counter-movements' that necessarily arise to limit the cancerous effects of capitalism. The question is whether these collective regulations are designed to buttress the privileges of the elites, if they are reactionary, identitarian or totalitarian, or whether they will offer an opportunity to deepen democracy and enlightenment.

In particular, Polanyi interpreted the explosive political situation of the inter-war period as the result of a dispute between different post-liberal projects that competed to establish their respective versions of market limits. On the one hand, the type of dynamic that Gramsci described as 'passive revolution': authoritarian interventions that proposed aggressive institutional transformations, including economic regulation, with the objective of preserving the inherited system of stratification. On the other hand, a spectrum of democratizing currents that sought to impel processes of de-commercialization in order to reduce inequality and advance on a path of emancipation.

The present situation offers significant analogies with the political polarization, institutional instability and collective hatred that Polanyi experienced first-hand. In a certain sense, we are already living in post-neoliberal societies. The ideal of the free market is a political zombie that continues to cause suffering and emit inarticulate sounds, but which everyone takes for dead. Throughout the world, powerful counter-movements are arising in reaction to the neoliberal dystopia. The majority of these move in the orbit of the far right, of identitarian nationalism, xenophobia, religious fundamentalism and reactionary populism. Western political institutions are ceasing to act as mediators of democratic deliberation, and having an anabolic effect on the brutalization of public discourse, de-legitimizing political discussion by reducing it to questions of security. The 'illiberal democracy' that the Hungarian prime minister Viktor Orbán proclaimed in 2014, and the victory of Donald Trump in 2016, are spectacular manifestations of a dynamic that already affects all Western countries to a lesser or greater degree. To give one example, when Trump's proposal to build a wall between Mexico and the United States is criticized, people carefully overlook the fact that on the European Union's only land frontier with Africa – the Spanish territories in northern Morocco – there has already been for several years a triple metal fence, six metres high and topped with razor wire, which has caused horrific injuries to hundreds of immigrants.

Fortunately, reactionary counter-movements are only one side of the story. There are also democratizing and egalitarian alternatives that aspire to take advantage of the window of opportunity opened by the economic crisis in order to impel far-reaching social transformations on the basis of transnational solidarity. If in the early years of the present century Latin America was the motor of global opposition, continuing the alterglobalist movement that arose from the Seattle protests of 1999,[4] perhaps today we need to look for new laboratories of counter-hegemony in the semi-peripheral countries of southern Europe.

Learning from the European periphery

What is certain is that the economic recession is having explosive political effects in Mediterranean Europe. It has transformed the polite and conflict-free postmodern depoliticization – diagnosed and defended by authors such as Anthony Giddens and Ronald Inglehart – into a major crisis of legitimacy.[5] In Spain, especially, it has shattered a political regime based on the alternation of power between two majority parties whose programmes were the same in basic essentials, such as the deregulation of the labour market and the limitation of redistributive policies.[6] The legitimacy of this bipartisan regime derived from an economy of growth based on the housing market, which offered the promise of upward social mobility and high consumption capacity. To a large extent this was a mirage, as levels of unemployment, precariousness and inequality remained very high, and the welfare state had little redistributive effect. But for a long while, it was a very effective source of social cohesion.

The economic crisis exploded this consensus. The dream of the housing boom turned into a speculative nightmare, characterized by massive unemployment (in Spain there are more than four million unemployed, and a million and a half families with no member in work), poverty (one in three children is at risk of poverty or exclusion) and eviction (half a million since the start of the crisis). The countless cases of political corruption are viewed by Spanish citizens as the symptom of a deep institutional crisis induced by connivance between economic and political elites. Social discontent became visible in spring 2011 with the eruption of the 15M movement (the *indignados*) and the cycle of mobilizations that this unleashed. But the great change happened in 2014, when this movement managed to storm the political institutions. In the first place, Podemos shook the political landscape by winning 8 per cent of the votes in the elections to the European Parliament. A few months later, municipal candidates who sprang from the popular initiatives around 15M were victorious in many Spanish localities. At the present time, the three largest Spanish cities – Madrid, Barcelona and Valencia – are governed by initiatives for change, with a strongly critical and anti-commercialist slant.

This oppositional dynamic has been surprising and a cause of hope; as Owen Jones has noted, the models of mobilization and political intervention that have appeared in Spain may be repeatable in other countries.[7] In contrast to what has happened elsewhere, for the time being the Spanish reaction to the crisis has scarcely had any xenophobic or authoritarian character. It is not easy to explain this immunity, which is most likely due to a combination of different factors: the still fresh memory of dictatorship, the strong family solidarity that has mitigated economic suffering, and the integration of part of the far right into the major conservative party. But also crucial has been the appearance of movements that have succeeded in channelling discontent and indignation into a claim for the deepening of democracy, transforming the traditional discourse of the left to reach out to a social majority. In fact, it is certainly no exaggeration to maintain that in Spain we have seen a tentative normalization of positions that until recently were current only on the periphery of social movements. Today, feminism, social economics and participative democracy have a much greater public visibility than before the crisis.[8]

In fact, the question that has to be posed is why the process of political change has not been more rapid and deep. How is it possible that seven million Spaniards continue to vote for a conservative government that has carried out the greatest social cuts of the democratic period and is completely riven by cases of corruption? Part of the answer undoubtedly has to do with the brutal and successful effort made by all the mass communications media to demonize the supporters of change. But it is also clear that the left has many difficulties in putting forward an alternative political model able to overcome a logic of ideological discourse and address a

social majority on questions related to their material conditions of life.

The social crisis and the limits of
middle-classness

The 15M movement, Podemos and the other Spanish transformative movements have stood at the gates of workplaces
and been incapable of generating a class solidarity based on
shared precariousness that would overcome micro-identities
based on housing assets or social and cultural capital.[9] Mobilization based on indignation at the economic crisis, inequality and corruption has not been translated into proposals for
an alternative social model that is not just of theoretical interest to university professors or ideological interest to activists,
but that offers the majority of people a realistic alternative of a good life for which it is worthwhile taking risky
political decisions. In Spain as in other countries, resistance
to 'austericide' has been led by what are sociologically the
middle classes, whose indignation has less to do with immediate material suffering than with an 'existential' discontent
– meaning the closure of expectations of upward mobility
and the failure to keep social promises made in the past. This
is a limited motor of political change, strongly marked by a
loss-aversion tendency.

There is an old Marxist idea that may well be worth repeating here. Marx believed that the losers from capitalism are the
privileged agents of political change. They are the only ones in
a condition to impel certain moral advances that would benefit
everyone but that no other group can champion because they
are all caught up in their particular immediate interests. For
example, many people think that in a highly technological
society it would be rational to stop treating employment as
a scarce good that we have to compete for, and to look for
political alternatives that would enable us to convert the
problem of unemployment into a solution – concretely, into
a source of free time and the revaluation of reproductive
work. But those among us who cling on to precarious jobs are
little disposed to assume the costs and risks of the transition
to a more sensible system, as this could involve substantial

damage in the short term. We are capable of imagining this social reorganization and appreciating its advantages, but to actively support it we would have to become moral heroes prepared to immolate ourselves on the altar of political rationality. On the other hand, if you are twenty years old, your whole family has been unemployed for five years, and the rate of youth unemployment in your community is 70 per cent, the destruction of the labour market as we know it can more easily seem to you a feasible and moderate plan.

The moral is that emancipatory projects urgently require a break with the social confinement of progressive discourse to the zone of the middle classes, sometimes disguised as theoretical radicalism. Contrary to what the traditional workerist left suggests, however, this is not an ideological problem – the alienation of the proletariat or the frivolity of a 'caviar left' – but has to do with the social conditions of political change. Contemporary emancipatory initiatives take place on a devastated social terrain. The true victory of neoliberalism was to ravage civil society and convert us into a fragile, individualist and consumerist society.

In 1987, Margaret Thatcher uttered in an interview her famous words 'There is no such thing as society.' Many people interpreted this as an expression of methodological individualism. In actual fact, it was a political programme. This was understood much better by communitarian authors such as Richard Sennett or Christopher Lasch than by the heirs of Marx.[10] The global rout of the trade unionism of the 1980s not only meant a dramatic decline in the negotiating power of the workers, but was above all the culmination of the destruction of a wide complex of spaces of socialization directly involved in processes of material subsistence of the popular classes. In contrast, the upper classes managed to shield themselves from postmodern individualization by preserving their social capital – for example, through elite educational establishments or affinity networks bound up with lifestyle – a simulacrum of a cultural project, based on sophisticated consumption. Today the possibilities of success for emancipatory counter-movements require the reconstruction of universalist social bonds in which material sustenance has a crucial weight – not only paid employment, but also reproductive and care work.

Globally learned defencelessness and the possibility of Europe

A second restraint on the emerging counter-hegemonies consists in what could be called a kind of globally learned defencelessness. The dynamics of contemporary capitalism do not necessarily entail a lack of mechanisms of international political cooperation, but they are based on its absence. In the Western democracies, global markets vote, and their vote weighs more than those of parliaments. The most recent case is certainly that of Greece. In 2015, when the Greeks committed the mistake of making the 'wrong' electoral choice, the EU put in place a sadistic machinery of financial, political and media warfare designed to convert this decision into a continental lesson in political discipline.

It will be difficult today for a project of democratization to succeed in convincing a social majority if it is unable to overcome this learned defencelessness by proposing realistic mechanisms for recovering political sovereignty. One of these is certainly the extension of the geographical frame of constituent intervention beyond the frontiers of the nation-state; in other words, the construction of transnational alliances able to challenge the power of the global plutocracy. The good news is that, in contrast to the situation under classical internationalism, today in Europe something of this kind is more than a pious proposal, as we already have at our disposal the embryo of a continental institutional framework. Still more, the transnational space of political intervention that counter-hegemonic movements require could be the last hope for the project of European unity, which since the start of the crisis has been experiencing an accelerated process of decomposition.

The defence of the European Union made today is largely a kind of low-intensity continental nationalism, involving sanctimonious, outmoded and affected apologias for the European cultural legacy and for our ridiculous propensity – the very limit of black humour – to arrogate the role of the world's moral gendarme. In fact, if Europe matters it is not because it is Europe but, on the contrary, because – despite all adherence to European political, social and cultural traditions

– the continental union could constitute a step in the construction of forms of post-capitalist global cooperation. This
is certainly an idea that runs against the European institutional architecture. From its origin, the EU has understood
itself as a successful realization of the principle of commercial
pacification, an old theory that goes back to the Enlightenment and maintains that trade generates cordiality among
peoples whereas politics and culture drive them to conflict.[11]
Under the shock of the religious wars that made Europe a
killing ground, Montesquieu and other writers believed that
shared economic interests could help to overcome quarrels
based on identity.

For almost forty years, this theory appeared to work. The
EU was a successful experiment and proof of the pacifying
power of the market, able to anticipate and prepare the ground
for the process of political convergence. In reality, however,
this was basically a myth. The commercialization of Europe's
international relations was balanced by a strong consensus
around the partial de-commercialization of labour-power at
the national level. In other words, up until the late 1970s,
European commercial unity developed at the same time as
the European welfare state, and this synchrony was the key
to its success. This was a process, moreover, that counted on
very strong support from the United States, which correctly
viewed Keynesian policies as a containing dyke against Soviet
expansion. After the end of the Cold War, as the welfare state
was increasingly challenged by neoliberal hegemony, the EU
turned out to be an empty financial carcass, in which the
decision to establish a single currency without common fiscal
and social policies amounted to slow-motion suicide.

The only escape from the implosion of the European
Union lies in undoing the historic mistake that gave priority
to the market in the construction of a continental political project. Only the democratizing counter-movements in
southern Europe are in a position to promote such a project.
As against the traditional political parties, they aspire to a
popular empowerment capable of ending the dictatorship
of the markets. And as distinct from identitarian or neo-
protectionist programmes such as Brexit, they require a
broadened frame of sovereignty that will permit them to
stand up successfully to the global economic elites that have

escaped the control of national states. Moreover, such a de-commercialization on the European scale could pose a strong challenge to the global neoliberal order. This was an argument made many years ago by the British political scientist Peter Gowan.[12] The European Union as a whole is the largest economy in the world, and the countries composing it have solid democratic political traditions. For this reason, Gowan suggested, it is in a position to lead a post-capitalist globalization: more just, more democratic and more prosperous.

Beyond the recession, beyond capitalism

The conversion of the precariat into a 'class for itself' with transformative potential, by way of new mechanisms of socialization and the creation of an international popular alliance, may seem a titanic project bordering on the utopian. In reality, this is the easy part of the contemporary emancipation programme. It will be still more difficult to break with the consensual logic that is dominant even in the most successful oppositional initiatives.

Certainly, one of the major political advances of recent decades has been the recuperation by social movements of the concept of democracy as a vital and challenging political ideal. Overcoming the traditional conception of oppositional politics as a heroic activity within the reach of only a handful of athletic activists well trained in a range of theoretical niceties is excellent news. The most vigorous popular movements across the world are those that have understood how radical the demand for normality can be. To seek to lead a more or less conventional life, to form a family, to have the opportunity to live in the district where you were born, to study something for which you have an aptitude, to trust public institutions and have the opportunity to take part in them – all this requires a complete change in the world as we know it.

But it is also true, as Anselm Jappe has pointed out, that the rhetoric of the 99 per cent against the 1 per cent is deeply fallacious, and has conveyed the idea that political change can be peaceful and free of conflict. As if by increasing taxes on the richest and improving public services we would already have set out on the path of social transformation by way of a more solidaristic and green alter-capitalism, a kind of Keynesian restoration for the twenty-first century. Sometimes we have even seen post-capitalism as a kind of capitalism without capitalists, as if our society were pregnant with solidarity and only required a few small adjustments to scale up present-day cooperative practices, especially those bound up with digital technology. This has never been the case and is even less so today, faced as we are with apocalyptic environmental perspectives. Far more than the collapse of capitalism, we should fear its success.

Richard Tawney once said that the true language of political transformation is not that of rights but that of duties. He also wrote that 'Democracy is unstable as a political system as long as it remains a political system and nothing more, instead of being, as it should be, not only a form of government but a type of society, and a manner of life which is in harmony with that type.'[13] I believe that this idea contains a profound truth, expressed in similar terms by Simone Weil and other Christian socialists of the inter-war period. Perhaps this offers us a kind of orientation that might avoid the blind alleys of both revolutionary epic and consensual paralysis.

Among a good part of the left that describes itself as 'responsible', averse to risky political aspirations and abrupt change, there is a dominant feeling today of nostalgia for the recent past, the good old days of New Labour and 'globalization with a human face'. But this would seem a perfect recipe for accelerating the economic, social and political crisis. The great recession is not so much a break in the way the West has organized itself over the last forty years as the result of various reactive attempts to reformulate this inherited order with the object of maintaining the privileges of the dominant classes. If we want to avoid catastrophe, we have to pass from the radicalization of normality to the normalization of a break, which means assuming that the conflict is opened not only against the handful of winners in the global economic casino but also against those aspects of our life that participate in capitalist barbarism.

Translated by David Fernbach

Notes

1 Robert Castel, *La montée des incertitudes. Travail, protections, statut de l'individu*, Paris: Seuil, 2009.

2 David Harvey, *A Brief History of Neoliberalism*, Oxford: Oxford University Press, 2007.

3 Karl Polanyi, *The Great Transformation: The Political and Economic Origins of Our Times*, Boston: Beacon Press, 2001 [1944].

4 James Petras, *The Left Strikes Back: Class and Conflict in the Age of Neoliberalism*, New York: Perseus, 1999.

5 Anthony Giddens, *Modernity and Self-Identity*, Stanford: Stanford University Press, 1991; Ronald Inglehart and Christian Welzel, *Modernization, Cultural Change, and Democracy*, Cambridge: Cambridge University Press, 2005.

6 In the northern European countries the popular legend has arisen that the Spanish economic crisis was caused by the pilfering of public funds and irresponsible economic policies. The truth is that until 2007 Spain was a model of liberal economic orthodoxy, with a debt of around 35 per cent of GDP (in the same year, the German debt was above 60 per cent). The Spanish debt rose precipitously after the crisis, when the government maintained against all odds the policy of containing public expenditure and submitted to the 'austericide' imposed by the European Union.

7 Owen Jones, 'There is a Model For the New Politics We Need. It's in Spain', *Guardian*, 22 June 2016.

8 Pew Research Global, 'Emerging and Developing Economies Much More Optimistic than Rich Countries about the Future', 8 September 2014; Fundación BBVA, 'Values and Worldviews', 5 April 2013.

9 There is the suspicion among other sectors of the European left that Podemos and other movements of change in Spain are slipping towards the political space of right-wing populism. For the moment, at least, this is a complete misunderstanding. The Podemos programme almost completely matches those of traditional transformative left parties. Besides, attempts to broaden its electoral base using a language with little ideological connotation – the opposition between the 'caste' and the 'people below', or appeals to patriotism – have had only limited success, and surveys show that political identity continues to play a crucial role among its voters.

10 Richard Sennett, *The Corrosion of Character: The Personal Consequences of Work in the New Capitalism*, New York: Norton,

1998; Christopher Lasch, *The Minimal Self: Psychic Survival in Troubled Times*, New York: Norton, 1984.

11 Albert O. Hirschman, *The Passions and the Interests: Political Arguments for Capitalism Before Its Triumph*, Princeton: Princeton University Press, 1977.

12 Peter Gowan, *The Globalization Gamble: The Dollar–Wall Street Regime and its Consequences*, London: Verso, 1999.

13 R. H. Tawney, *Equality*, London: Allen and Unwin, 1931, p. xvii.

13

The return of the repressed as the beginning of the end of neoliberal capitalism

Wolfgang Streeck

Neoliberalism arrived with globalization or else globalization arrived with neoliberalism; that is how the Great Regression began.[1] In the 1970s, the capital of the rebuilt industrial nations started to work its way out of the national servitude in which it had been forced to spend the decades following 1945.[2] The time had come to take leave of the tight labour markets, stagnant productivity, falling profits and increasingly ambitious demands of trade unions under a mature, state-administered capitalism. The road to the future, to a new expansion as is always close to the heart of capital, led outwards, to the still pleasantly unregulated world of a borderless global economy in which markets would no longer be locked into nation-states, but nation-states into markets.

The neoliberal about-face was presided over by a new goddess by the name of TINA – There is No Alternative. The long list of its high priests and priestesses extends from Margaret Thatcher via Tony Blair down to Angela Merkel. Anyone who wished to serve TINA to the accompaniment of the solemn chorus of the united economists of the world had to recognize the escape of capital into the world as both inevitable and beneficial, and would have to commit themselves to help clear all obstacles from its path. Heathen practices such as controls on the movement of capital, state aid and others would have to be tracked down and eradicated;

no one must be allowed to escape from 'global competition' and sink back into the cushioned comfort of national protections of whatever kind. Free trade agreements were to open up markets and protect them from state interference, global governance was to replace national governments, protection from commodification was to be replaced by enabling commodification, and the welfare state was to give way to the competition state of a new era of capitalist rationalization.[3]

By the end of the 1980s at the latest, neoliberalism had become the *pensée unique* of both the centre left and the centre right. The old political controversies were regarded as finished. Attention now focused on the 'reforms' needed to increase national 'competitiveness', and these reforms were everywhere the same. They included more flexible labour markets, improved 'stimuli' (positive at the upper end of the income distribution and negative at the bottom end), privatization, marketization as a weapon in the competition for location and cost reduction and as a test of moral endurance. Distributional conflict was replaced by a technocratic search for the economically necessary and uniquely possible; institutions, policies and ways of life were to be adapted to this end. All this was accompanied by the attrition of political parties – their retreat into the machinery of the state as 'cartel parties'[4] – with falling membership and declining electoral participation, disproportionately so at the lower end of the social scale in the 1980s, followed by the meltdown of trade union organization, together with a dramatic decline in strike activity worldwide – altogether, in other words, a demobilization along the broadest possible front of the entire post-war machinery of democratic participation and redistribution. It all took place slowly but steadily, developing into a new normal state of affairs.

As a process of institutional and political regression, the neoliberal revolution inaugurated a new age of *post-factual politics*.[5] This had become necessary because neoliberal globalization was far from actually delivering the prosperity for all that it had promised.[6] The inflation of the 1970s and the unemployment that accompanied its harsh elimination were followed by a rise in government debt in the 1980s and the restoration of public finances by 'reforms' of the welfare state in the 1990s. These in turn were followed, as compensation, by the generation of generous opportunities for private households to access credit and get indebted. Simultaneously, growth rates declined, although or because inequality and aggregate debt levels kept increasing. Instead of *trickle-down* there was the most vulgar sort of *trickle-up*: growing income inequality between individuals, families, regions and, in the Eurozone, nations. The promised service economy and knowledge-based society turned out to be smaller than the industrial society that was fast disappearing; hence a constant expansion of the numbers of people who were no longer needed, the surplus population of a revived capitalism on the move, watching helplessly and uncomprehendingly the transformation of the tax state into the debt state and finally into the consolidation state, and at the financial crises and the subsequent rescue programmes as a result of which they found themselves worse and worse off.[7] 'Global governance' didn't help, nor did the national democratic state that had become uncoupled from the capitalist economy for the sake of globalization. To make sure that this did not become a threat to the Brave New World of neoliberal capitalism, sophisticated methods were required to secure popular consent and disorganize would-be resisters. And in fact, the techniques developed for this purpose proved impressively effective initially.

The 'post-factual age'

Lies, even blatant lies, have always existed in politics. We need think only of Colin Powell's PowerPoint presentation to the United Nations Security Council, with his aerial photographs proving the existence of Iraqi weapons of mass destruction. As to Germany, one still remembers a defence minister, greatly revered up to this point as a social democrat of the old school, who claimed that the German troops sent into Afghanistan at the urging of the US were defending, 'at the Hindu Kush', the security of Germany. However, with the neoliberal revolution and the transition to 'post-democracy'[8] associated with it, a new sort of political deceit was born, the *expert lie*. It began with the Laffer Curve, which was used to prove scientifically that reductions in taxation lead to higher tax receipts.[9] It was followed, *inter alia*, by the European Commission's 'Cecchini Report' (1988), which, as a reward for the 'completion of the internal market' planned for 1992, promised the citizens of Europe an increase in prosperity of the order of 5 per cent of the European Union's GDP, an average 6 per cent reduction in the price of consumer goods, as well as 'millions of new jobs' and an improvement in public finances of 2.2 per cent of GDP. In the US, meanwhile, financial experts such as Bernanke, Greenspan and Summers agreed that the precautions taken by rational investors in their own interest and on their own account to stabilize ever 'freer' and ever more global financial markets were enough and that government agencies had no need to take action to prevent the growth of bubbles, partly because they had now learned how to eliminate painlessly the consequences if bubbles were to burst.

At the same time, the 'narratives'[10] disseminated by mainstream parties, governments and PR specialists and the decisions and non-decisions associated with them became ever more absurd. The penetration of the machinery of government by previous and future Goldman Sachs managers continued apace, in recognition of their indispensable expertise, as if nothing had changed. After seven years, in which not a single one of the bank managers who had shared responsibility for the crash of 2008 had been brought to justice, Obama's attorney general, Eric Holder, returned to the New York law firm from which he had come and to a princely million-dollar salary – a film specializing in the defence of banks and bankers against government prosecution. And Hillary Clinton, who together with her husband and daughter had amassed a fortune in the hundreds of millions in the sixteen years since leaving the White House, from Goldman Sachs speaking fees among other things, far above the earnings even of a Larry Summers, entered the election campaign as the self-designated representative of the 'hard-working middle class', a class that in reality had long since been reduced by capitalist progress to the status of a surplus population.

From the perspective of neoliberal internationalism, of course, which had developed the propagation of illusions into the fine art of democratic government, the post-factual age began as late as 2016, the year of the Brexit referendum and the smashing of Clintonism by Donald Trump.[11] Only after the collapse of post-democracy and the end of mass patience with the 'narratives' of a globalization that in the US had ultimately benefited solely the top 1 per cent did the guardians of the dominant 'discourse' call for obligatory fact-checking. Only then did they regret the 'deficits' experienced by those caught in the pincer grip of the global attention economy on the one hand and the cost-cutting in education on the other. It is at that point that they began to call for 'eligibility tests' of the most varied kind as a prerequisite for citizens being allowed to exercise their right to vote.[12] The fact that the Great Unwashed, who for so long had helped promote the progress of capitalism by passing their time with the Facebook pages of Kim Kardashian, Selena Gomez, Justin Bieber *e tutti quanti*, had now returned to the voting booth, appeared to be a sign of an ominous regression. Moreover, distractions in the form of 'humanitarian interventions' or the reanimation of the East–West conflict, this time with Russia instead of the USSR, and over LGBTQ instead of communism, seemed to have exhausted themselves. Truth and morality didn't matter anymore, and in England a Tory politician, when asked why he was campaigning to leave the EU against the advice of 'the experts', replied, 'People in this country have had enough of experts!'[13]

Moralization, demoralization and the return of the repressed

Characteristic of the 'intellectual situation of the age' today is a new cultural divide that has struck the capitalist democracies without warning. Structurally, it has its roots in long-festering discontent with 'globalization' while simultaneously the number of 'globalization losers' has been steadily growing. The process reached a tipping point in the years following the financial crisis of 2008 when the quantity of discontent transformed into the quality of open protest. One of the reasons why this took so long was that those who had earlier spoken up on behalf of society's losers joined the fan club of globalization, by the 1990s at the latest. For a while then, those experiencing 'globalization' as a problem rather than a solution had no one to speak on their behalf. Instead, the high phase of globalization sponsored the establishment of a cosmopolitan consciousness industry which discerned its opportunities for growth in turbocharging the expansionist drive of capitalist markets with the libertarian values of the social revolution of the 1960s and '70s and their utopian promise of human emancipation.[14] In the process, the technocratic *pensée unique* of neoliberalism became fused with the moral *juste milieu* of an internationalist discourse community. Its control over the airspace above the seminar desks serves today as operations base in a cultural struggle of a special kind, one in which the moralization of a globally expanding capitalism goes hand in hand with the demoralization of those who find their interests damaged by it.

After decades of decline, voter participation in the Western democracies has recently begun to bounce back, especially among the lower classes. The rediscovery of democracy as a political corrective, however, benefits exclusively new kinds of parties and movements whose appearance on the scene throws national political systems into disarray. The mainstream parties and their public relations experts, which have long become closely associated with each other and with the machinery of the state, regard the new parties as a lethal threat to 'democracy' and fight them as such. The concept employed in this struggle, one that has in the shortest of time been included in the post-factual vocabulary, is that of 'populism', denoting both left-wing and right-wing tendencies and organizations that reject the TINA logic of 'responsible' politics in a world of neoliberal globalization.

As a concept, 'populism' has a long history, one that goes back to the Progressive Era in the United States and to the Progressive Party of Robert M. La Follette (1855–1925; presidential candidate for the Progressive Party in 1924). Later on, populism was something of a neutral name for an ideology especially of Latin-American political movements, which saw themselves as representing 'the "people" in opposition to a self-selected and self-enriching "elite" '.[15] In recent years, the concept has been used by the parties and media of liberal internationalism all over the world as a general polemical term for the new opposition which is pressing for national alternatives to the internationalization declared to be without alternatives. The classical idea of populism is of a nation that constitutes itself in political conflicts as a united force to combat an economically powerful and culturally arrogant minority suppressing 'ordinary people'. As such, it could have either right-wing or left-wing connotations. This facilitated its appropriation by the globalizing faithful because it enables them to avoid distinctions, so that Trump and Sanders, Farage and Corbyn, and in Germany Petry and Wagenknecht can all be lumped together under the same heading.[16]

The fissure between those who describe others as 'populists' and those who are described by them as such is the dominant political fault line in the crisis-ridden societies of financial capitalism. The issue at stake is none other than the relationship between global capitalism and the state system. Nothing polarizes the capitalist societies of today more than the debates about the necessity and legitimacy of national politics. Here, interests and identities fuse and give rise to mutual declarations of hostility of an intensity such as we have not seen since the end of the Cold War. The resulting religious wars, which can at any moment escalate into moral annihilation campaigns, impinge on the deepest and most sensitive strata of social and individual identity where decisions are taken about respect and contempt, inclusion and exclusion, recognition and excommunication.[17]

What is significant about the politics of internationalization is the conformity with which those described as 'elites', contemptuously by the 'populists' and approvingly by themselves, react to the new parties. 'Populism' is diagnosed in normal internationalist usage as a cognitive problem. Its supporters are supposed to be people who demand 'simple solutions' because they do not understand the necessarily complex solutions that are so indefatigably and successfully delivered by the tried and tested forces of internationalism – and their representatives are cynics who promise 'the people' the 'simple solutions' they crave, even though they know that there are no alternatives to the complex solutions of the technocrats. In this way, the emergence of the new parties can be explained as a Great Regression on the part of the Little People, manifesting itself as a lack of both education and respect for the educated. This calls forth 'discourses' about the desirability of abolishing referendums or about handing political decisions over to unpolitical experts and authorities.

At the level of everyday life this leads to a moral and cultural exclusion of the anti-globalization parties and their supporters. The declaration of their cognitive immaturity is followed by moral denunciation of calls for a renewed national politics as a bulwark against the risks and side effects of internationalization. The relevant battle cry, which is to mobilize memories of racism and war, is 'ethno-nationalism'. 'Ethno-nationalists' are not up to the task of dealing with the challenges of globalization, neither the economic ones – 'global competition' – nor the moral ones. Their 'fears and concerns', as the official phrase puts it, 'are to be taken seriously', but only in the mode of social work. Protests against material and moral degradation are suspected of being fascist, especially now that the former advocates of the plebeian classes have switched to the globalization party, so that if their former clients wish to complain about the pressures of capitalist modernization, the only language at their disposal is the pre-political, untreated linguistic raw material of their everyday deprivation experience. This results in constant breaches of the rules of civilized public speech, which in turn can become a cause of indignation at the top as well as of mobilization at the bottom. In response, losers and refusers of internationalization elude moral censure by exiting from public media and entering the 'social media'. In this way they can make use of the most globalized of all infrastructures to build up their own, separatist, communication circles in which they need not fear being reprimanded for being culturally and morally backward.[18]

Cut off

Among the astonishing events of 2016 we must include the way in which Brexit and Trump surprised not just the liberal public but also its social sciences. Nothing documents better the division in the globalized societies of neoliberalism than the bafflement of their power and discourse elites at the sight of the return of the repressed, whose political apathy they had felt entitled to interpret as insightful resignation. Even the proverbially 'excellent' and correspondingly well-endowed universities of the east and west coasts of America had failed to serve as early-warning systems. Evidently, nothing much could be gleaned any more about the condition of the destabilized crisis societies of the present from opinion surveys conducted via twenty-minute telephone interviews. There seems to be a steady increase in the number of people who regard social scientists as spies from a foreign power who have to be avoided or, should that be impossible, whose disapproval one avoids by giving them the answers one believes are expected. In this way, the illusions of the 'elites' about the condition of their societies were pathologically confirmed. Only very few social scientists nowadays seem to be able to understand what lies beneath them; those who had read a book such as Robert Putman's *Our Kids: The American Dream in Crisis* could not have been surprised by Trump's victory.[19]

It will be a long time before the globally bourgeoisified left understands the events of 2016. In Great Britain the surviving Blair supporters in the Labour Party believed they could persuade their traditional voters to remain in the EU with a lengthy catalogue of the economic benefits of membership, without taking the uneven distribution of those benefits into account. It did not occur to a liberal public cut off from the everyday experience of the groups and regions in decline that the electorate might have wanted the government they had installed to show greater interest in their concerns than in international agreements. And there were plenty of voters who simply did not understand that international solidarity among workers in the twenty-first century should mean that it was their duty to open up their own job to unrestrained global competition.

Interregnum

What are we to expect now? Trump's demolition of the Clinton machine, Brexit and the failure of Hollande and Renzi – all in the same year – mark a new phase in the crisis of the capitalist state system as transformed by the neoliberal revolution. To describe this phase I have proposed Antonio

Gramsci's term 'interregnum',[20] a period of uncertain dura-
tion in which an old order is dying but a new one cannot yet
be born. The old order that was destroyed by the onslaught
of the populist barbarians in 2016 was the world of globalized capitalism. Its governments had neutralized their
national democracies in post-democratic fashion so as not to
lose touch with the global expansion of capital, putting off
demands for democratic and egalitarian interventions in capitalist markets by referring them to a global democracy of the
future. What the still to be created new order will look like
is an open question, as is to be expected of an interregnum.
Until it comes into being, according to Gramsci, we have to
accept that 'a great variety of morbid symptoms will appear'.

An interregnum in Gramsci's sense is a period of great
uncertainty in which familiar chains of cause and effect are no
longer in force and unexpected, dangerous and grotesquely
abnormal events may occur at any moment. This is in part
because disparate lines of development run unreconciled
parallel to each other, resulting in unstable configurations,
and chains of *surprising events* take the place of *predictable
structures*. Among the causes of the new unpredictability is
the fact that, following the populist revolution, the political
classes of neoliberal capitalism are forced to listen rather
more closely to their national populations. After decades in
which national democracies were hung out to dry in favour
of institutions that promoted globalization, they are now
coming back into their own as channels for the articulation
of discontent. The times are now past for the planned demolition of lines of national defence in the face of the rational-
izing pressure of international markets. Trump's victory has
already ruled out a second referendum in Great Britain on the
EU model according to which referendums are repeated until
they produce the right answer. A re-awakened electorate will
no more go along with supposed economic necessities with
no alternative than it will acquiesce in claims that border
controls are technically impossible. Parties that have relied
on *responsibility* will have to relearn what *responsiveness*
means[21] or else they will have to give way to other parties.

The 'One Nation' rhetoric of the new British prime minister shows that this has not escaped the attention of at least
part of the political leadership. As early as her speech on

11 July 2016, launching her prime ministerial campaign, May called for changes that had not been heard of since the 1980s, not even from the Labour Party: war on inequality, fairer taxation of higher incomes, a better education system, workers on company boards, protection for British jobs against offshoring, and all that together with limits on immigration. The fact that the vote for Britain's exit from the EU has reminded British politicians that their first responsibility is to their electorate is evident also in May's speech in November 2016 to the Confederation of British Industry, in which she explained the result of the referendum in terms of people's 'wish for a stronger, fairer country'.

May's neo-protectionist programme poses awkward questions for the social-democratic left. Trump, too, if he tried to make good on his industrial and fiscal policy promises, might become a problem for the left, and in fact the canny Bernie Sanders has already offered him his support several times, both for the rehabilitation of the old industrial regions that continued to decay during the eight Obama years and also for a 'Keynesian' programme to rebuild the nation's infrastructure. The increase in debt this would require, especially if the promised tax cuts are implemented, would fit the neo-Keynesian recipes that have been long favoured by politicians and economists of the moderate left ('end of austerity'). Given the resistance of the remnants of the Tea Party, these are measures that could be passed by Congress only with Democratic assistance. The same would hold for the use of 'helicopter money', another measure apparently contemplated by Trump, which would require in addition the cooperation of the Federal Reserve.

To be sure, even a post-globalist, neo-protectionist policy of the kind envisaged by Trump and May, and soon perhaps also by Le Pen or Hamon, will be unable to guarantee stable growth, more and better quality employment, a deleveraging of both public and private debt, or trust in the dollar or the euro. The financialized crisis capitalism of the present is no more governable nationally from below than internationally from above. It hangs by the silken thread of an 'unconventional' monetary policy, which is attempting to create something like growth by negative interest rates and an adventurous expansion of the money supply, engineered

through 'quantitative easing' – the purchase of bonds by the
central banks with freshly created cash. The neoliberal structural reforms that the 'experts' think would be the essential
complement to this have been foiled in the countries where
they actually might be of some use by popular resistance to
the 'globalization' of their ways of life. At the same time,
economic inequality is on the rise partly because trade unions
and states have lost their power or ceded it to the global
markets. The utter destruction of national institutions capable
of economic redistribution and the resultant over-reliance on
monetary and central bank policy as the economic policy of
last resort have made capitalism ungovernable, whether by
'populist' or technocratic methods.

Domestic conflicts can also be foreseeable where cultural
symbols are concerned. Will the enhanced 'populist' valua-
tion of the natives require a devaluation of immigrants in the
broadest sense? And can the left succeed in paying a credible
cultural tribute to those woken up from their apathy? Too
many angry words have been exchanged, quite apart from
the fact that any reconciliation might well alienate the left's
bourgeoisified supporters in the cosmopolitan middle class.
And in the event of economic setbacks, Trump, May and
others will be tempted to deflect criticism by launching more
or less subtle campaigns against ethnic and other minorities.
Rebellions of the decent as well as the indecent would be the
consequence.

On the international plane, matters might be less dramatic, at least initially. Unlike Obama, Blair and Clinton, also
Sarkozy, Hollande, Cameron, and perhaps even Merkel, the
'last defender of the free West',[22] the new national protectionists have no great human rights ambitions, whether in China
and Russia or, so far as one can tell, in Africa or the Middle
East. Anyone in favour of humanitarian intervention in the
broadest sense may well regret this. Lack of Russian appre-
ciation for artists such as Pussy Riot is unlikely to trigger
missionary reflexes in the inward-turned governments of the
period after Trump's election victory. In the United States
Victoria Nuland ('Fuck the EU') was not made Secretary of
State after all, and the Human Rights faction of the State
Department have now returned to their university chairs.
Plans to draw Ukraine into the EU and NATO and thereby

to deprive the Russians of their Black Sea navy port are now off the table, as are any 'regime change' projects in countries such as Syria. Of course China could conceivably take Russia's place, since a President Trump will have to persuade it to give up market share in the US while continuing to buy and hold US Treasury bills.

In the under-structured context of the beginning interregnum with its dysfunctional institutions and chaotic causal chains, the 'populists' will be an additional source of uncertainty as they make inroads into the machinery of the state. The onset of the interregnum appears as a Bonapartist moment: everything is possible, but nothing has consequences, least of all the intended ones, because in the neoliberal revolution society has reverted to the condition of 'a sack of potatoes'.[23] The new protectionists will not put an end to the crisis of capitalism; but they will bring politics back into play and will remind it of the middle and lower strata of the population who have been the losers from globalization. The left too, or what has become of it, has no idea how the ungovernable capitalism of the present can make the transition to a better ordered, less endangered and less dangerous future – see Hollande, Renzi, Clinton. But if it has any wish again to play a part in this, it must learn its lessons from the failure of 'global governance' and the ersatz politics of identity. Among them are: that the outcasts of the self-appointed 'knowledge society' must not be abandoned for aesthetic reasons to their fate and, hence, to the right; that cosmopolitanism at the expense of 'ordinary people' cannot be enforced in the long run even with neoliberal means of coercion; and that the national state can be opened up only *with* its citizens and not *against* them. Applying this to Europe, this means that whoever wants too much integration will reap only conflict and end up with less integration. The cosmopolitan identitarianism of the leaders of the neoliberal age, originating as it did in part from left-wing universalism, calls forth by way of reaction a national identitarianism, while anti-national re-education from above produces an anti-elitist nationalism from below. Whoever puts a society under economic or moral pressure to the point of dissolution meets with resistance from traditionalists. This is because all those who find themselves exposed to the uncertainties of international markets, control of which has been promised but never delivered, will prefer the bird in their hand to two in the bush: they will choose the reality of national democracy over the fantasy of a democratic global society.

Translated by Rodney Livingstone

Notes

1 As will become even clearer below, concepts such as this one, which have become fixtures of the repertoire of political rhetoric, are being employed here against the grain.
2 Wolfgang Streeck, *Buying Time: The Delayed Crisis of Democratic Capitalism*, translated by Patrick Camiller, London and New York: Verso, 2014 [2013].
3 Wolfgang Streeck, 'Industrielle Beziehungen in einer internationalisierten Wirtschaft', in Ulrich Beck (ed.), *Politik der Globalisierung*, Frankfurt am Main: Suhrkamp, 1998, pp. 169–202.
4 Peter Mair and Richard S. Katz, 'Changing Models of Party Organization and Party Democracy: The Emergence of the Cartel Party', *Party Politics*, 1:1 (1995), pp. 5–28.
5 See note 1, above.
6 On the following see Streeck, *Buying Time*.
7 Oliver Nachtwey, *Die Abstiegsgesellschaft. Über das Aufbegehren in der regressiven Moderne*, Berlin: Suhrkamp, 2016 (English translation forthcoming).
8 Colin Crouch, *Post-Democracy*, Cambridge: Polity, 2004.
9 For the contribution of the economist Arthur B. Laffer to Reaganite taxation and government debt policies, see David A. Stockman, *The Triumph of Politics: How the Reagan Revolution Failed*, New York: Harper and Row, 1986.
10 This term has recently migrated from literary theory and psychology into politics, where it has made a meteoric career. No wonder. According to Wikipedia, a narrative is a 'meaningful story in which emotions are transported and which provides an orientation and conveys confidence'. See https://de.wikipedia. org/wiki/Narrativ (retrieved November 2016). This concept is especially popular nowadays with reference to 'Europe', where every time an election goes awry, self-appointed 'Europeans' call for 'a better narrative'.
11 On 15 November 2016, the editor of the Oxford Dictionaries announced that 'post-truth' had been nominated Word of the Year. This was followed immediately by the Society for the

German Language, which declared 'post-factual' ['postfaktisch']
to be the German Word of the Year. 'Ever larger sections of the
population' were said to be ready 'in their feelings of resentment towards "those up there" to ignore the facts and are even
prepared to accept obvious lies. It is not the claim to truth, but
the expression of a "felt truth" that brings success in the "post-
factual age".' After decades of constructivist hegemony in the
faculties of literature (see 'narrative'!), a sudden rediscovery
of objective truth for the purpose of insulting non-academic
fellow-citizens.

12 The similarity to the literacy tests to which people with dark
    skins used to be subjected in the Southern US states is strik-
    ing. On 29 November 2016 in an article in the *Frankfurter
    Allgemeine Zeitung*, Sandro Gaycken, 'Director of the Digital
    Society Institute', which, according to its website, is 'a strategic
    research institute for digital topics of the German DAX compa-
    nies', wrote: 'We need a "gnosocracy". Whoever wants to vote
    must demonstrate political competence ... To do this, every poll
    booth must be provided with a variable multiple-choice test,
    with simple questions from every sphere: external, internal, the
    environment, the economy, etc. Whoever passes the test, may
    vote.'

13 Michael Gove, quoted in Henry Mance, 'Britain Has Had Enough
    of Experts, Says Gove', *Financial Times*, 3 June 2016, at https://
    www.ft.com/content/3be49734-29cb-11e6-83e4-abc22d5d108c
    (retrieved November 2016).

14 This is one facet of the way in which '1968' was co-opted by a
    capitalism eager to adapt itself to an altered society, as described
    by Luc Boltanski and Ève Chiapello in *The New Spirit of Capi-
    talism*, translated by Gregory Elliott, London and New York:
    Verso, 2006.

15 Ernesto Laclau, *On Populist Reason*, London and New York:
    Verso, 2005; Chantal Mouffe, *Agonistics: Thinking The World
    Politically*, London and New York: Verso, 2013.

16 The 'populists' retaliate by describing all adherents to the TINA
    doctrine, regardless of their origins, as an indistinguishably
    uniform globalization 'elite'.

17 The international dimension of this conflict is interesting. The
    Internationalist International warns against the *Nationalist
    International*, which it wants to see combated by all in the
    name of democracy – and the same is true vice versa. Occa-
    sionally, we hear talk of an *Authoritarian International* to be
    fought by the *(Neo-)liberal International* in both domestic and
    foreign policy. (In this way nationalism and authoritarianism
    are equated.)

18 In Germany the Alternative für Deutschland has more Facebook followers than any other party.
19 Robert D. Putnam, *Our Kids: The American Dream in Crisis*, New York: Simon & Schuster, 2015.
20 Wolfgang Streeck, *How Will Capitalism End?*, London and New York: Verso, 2016, pp. 35–46.
21 Peter Mair, 'Representative versus Responsible Governments', MPIfG Working Paper, No. 09/8 (September 2009), at http://observgo.uquebec.ca/observgo/fichiers/88022_GRA-1.pdf (retrieved November 2016).
22 Alison Smale and Steven Erlanger, 'As Obama Exits World Stage, Angela Merkel May Be the Liberal West's Last Defender', *New York Times*, 12 November 2016, at www.nytimes.com/2016/11/13/world/europe/germany-merkel-trump-election.html (retrieved November 2016).
23 Karl Marx, *The Eighteenth Brumaire of Louis Bonaparte*, in Marx, *Surveys from Exile*, translated by Ben Fowkes, Harmondsworth: Penguin Books, 1973, p. 239. ['Thus the great mass of the French nation is formed by the simple addition of isomorphous magnitudes, much as potatoes in a sack form a sack of potatoes.' – Trans.]

14

Dear President Juncker

David Van Reybrouck

Dear President Juncker,

The European Union might be over very soon. Exit referendums, the rise of populism, the transformation of the transatlantic alliance, the new imperial ambitions of neighbouring Russia, the failure of the Arab Spring, the refugee crisis, terrorism, the overall loss of trust in the political establishment ... All these social and political developments of the past few years have brought about a rapid weakening of what seemed an encompassing and solid level of organizing public life.

Unprecedented in history, the European Union's trajectory over the past fifty years has been one of growing in size and in power. What started off as an elite project between two countries in the post-war years – 'let us connect the heavy steel industries of France and Germany so that they can no longer rearm without the other knowing it' – has become the most powerful level of political decision making for half a billion citizens. Truly, it has been an extraordinary project.

In November 2014, you were installed as the 12th president of the European Commission, together with the European Council the most important executive branch of power in Europe. You might become the last one, too.

A few years ago, a friend of mine, the Brussels-based artist Thomas Bellinck, constructed a temporary museum of the

European dream. 'Domo de Eŭropa Historio en Ekzilo' was
the title in Esperanto: the house of European history in exile.
Did you visit it? It presented itself as 'the first international
exhibition on life in the former European Union'. Taking
visitors 'more than half a century back in time to the early
twenty-first century', they could see the remains of a political project decades after it had collapsed. The museum itself
looked run-down and shabby, the sort of small-scale institution run by a few volunteers and collectors on Saturday after-
noons, a few sombre rooms filled with yellowing newspaper
clippings from the 2010s and dusty showcases with dead flies.
The first object the visitor could admire was a faded copy of
the Nobel Peace Prize given to the European Union a long
time ago, in the long-forgotten year of 2012. The museum,
which in reality was a very smart artistic installation, opened
its doors in Brussels, Vienna, Athens, Rotterdam, Wiesbaden,
and so on.

It all seemed a funny hyperbole, Mr Juncker, but the
artist was completely sincere about it: this entire remarkable
project might be over one day. Good art can sometimes be
visionary, but I wonder whether Thomas Bellinck could have
foreseen how fast the Great Regression would start to unfold.
In hindsight, the year 2016 might turn out to be the moment
when the tipping point was reached.

Ever since Brexit and Trump, we have seen thousands
of real-time analyses and commentaries. We could read all
about what was wrong with politicians, parties and even
people – but surprisingly very little on what was wrong
with procedures. It is still a heresy to ask whether elections,
in their current form, are a badly outmoded technology for
converting the collective will of the people into governments
and policies.

Since the Great Regression has many different origins, it
will inevitably require many different remedies. But in this
letter, I want to focus on one dimension I find extremely
important: the way we do democracy. I am interested in the
practical procedures and the mundane interfaces we use to
make democracy happen. To be sure, this has to do with my
background. I am an archaeologist by training: I believe that
the practical conditions of the material world are not just of
secondary importance, but constitute the world. Instruments

shape results. Or, as Churchill remarked when debating the question in which shape the House of Commons should be rebuilt after it had been destroyed by German bombs: 'We shape our buildings and afterwards our buildings shape us.'

In order to let people have their say, the instruments we typically have at our disposal are elections and referendums. Yet are these tools the best available? Are citizens who are invited to take major decisions on the future of their society at their best in the penumbra of the voting booth, behind a closed curtain, without any obligation to inform themselves or any formal chance to deliberate with others first? Is this old ritual of voting really the best we can come up with in the early twenty-first century in terms of collective decision making? Are these the most adequate means to let people express their dreams and policy preferences?

I really doubt so. And I would even argue that we urgently need to update our ways of doing democracy, by calling for a reform of procedures that might bring people back into the democratic process in order to cure some of the symptoms and maladies described above.

In an election, you may cast your vote, but you are also casting it away for the next few years. This system of delegation to an elected representative may have been necessary in the past – when communication was slow and information was limited – but it is completely out of touch with the way citizens interact with each other today.

Do we really need to stay with a procedure that dates back to the late eighteenth century, especially when it is so often perverted into a carnival of promises, sponsoring and spin? Is ticking a box next to someone's name really the best we can come up with in an age of information, communication and increased education? Elections are the fossil fuel of politics: once they gave a boost to democracy, now they generate a whole new series of dangers.

Referendums are hardly any better. In a referendum, we ask people directly what they think when they have not been obliged to think – although they have certainly been bombarded by every conceivable form of manipulation in the months leading up to the vote.

For several decades now, referendums have been propagated as a useful means to bridge the gap between citizens and politicians. With a referendum, the argument goes, the individual can reclaim some of the substantial power he or she typically gives away for several years in a traditional representative democracy. Citizens do not delegate the entirety of their decision making, but can have a say on particular policy issues in between two electoral moments. Yet rather than bridging the gap between those who govern and those who are governed, most recent referendums have created new and much deeper gaps. Brexit, the Dutch referendum on the association treaty with Ukraine, the Italian referendum on parliamentary reform, the Colombian referendum on the peace treaty with the FARC have all taught us one thing: if public consultation is reduced to a YES/NO question to be answered in the voting booth, referendums do not reunite countries, but divide them even further.

I fail to understand how complex policy issues such as membership of the EU or parliamentary reform can be solved through a single blow of the blunt axe of a referendum. I fail to understand how such constitutional heart surgery can be performed with a rusty instrument in the hand of citizens whose competence is uncertain.

Although the possibility of substantial participation is certainly an improvement compared with elections, referendums create new difficulties. First, there is no way of knowing whether citizens are informed or not. Even with a fair and balanced campaign devoid of any lies (a rarity these days), even with factual, objective information handed out by the government (as is the case in Switzerland), there is still no guarantee that those who vote are properly informed.

Second, there is no way of knowing why people vote one way or another. In a referendum, you often get an answer to a question that was not really asked. A specific policy proposal may be at stake, but a substantial section of the electorate may seize the opportunity to pass judgement on the overall performance of the government. So, referendums can sometimes function as mid-term evaluations or even early elections. Things become completely bizarre when heads of government like David Cameron or Matteo Renzi explicitly link their own political career to the outcome of a referendum. Apart from grossly overestimating their own popularity, these leaders muddle matters even more. In that case, you get an answer to a question that was explicitly raised, but that was not even on the ballot.

So, elections and referendums are both rather imperfect instruments for allowing people to express their political ideals. Both Brexit and Trump painfully illustrate the dangerous road that all Western democracies have taken: reducing democracy to voting.

If we refuse to update our democratic technology, we may find the system is beyond repair; 2016 has already become the worst year for democracy since 1933. Donald Trump is not an oddity, but the logical outcome of a democratic system that combines the eighteenth-century procedure of voting with the nineteenth-century idea of universal suffrage, the twentieth-century invention of mass media and the twenty-first-century culture of social media.

After the American and French revolutions, elections were not introduced to make democracy possible, but to empower a 'natural aristocracy', as Thomas Jefferson, one of the Founding Fathers of United States, called it. Power should no longer be in the hands of those with titles, castles and hunting grounds, but should be given to people who had distinguished themselves by their intellectual competence and moral excellence. The words 'elite' and 'elections' are etymologically related: elections are the procedure by which a new elite is created.

It has been the great contribution of the French philosopher Bernard Manin to unravel the aristocratic underpinnings of modern representative government.[1] In the nineteenth and twentieth centuries, the essentially aristocratic procedure of voting was democratized by extending the right to vote to more and more citizens: farmers, factory workers, women, younger people, newcomers. Yet this was more a process of quantitative than qualitative democratization: more and more people could vote, but the vast majority of citizens still could not speak. Ticking a box at periodic intervals was the only way the masses could express themselves to their governors.

Mass media like newspapers, radio and television were the key communication channels between citizens and politicians in the twentieth century. A remarkable commercialization of that media took place in the last quarter of the century, deeply transforming the structure and the nature of the public sphere. Between the top of the pyramid (those in power) and its base (the people), the intermediate zone was much less organized by civil society than by the workings of the media market.

The rise of the interactive internet in the early twenty-first century brought about a new fundamental change. Social media turned passive consumers of information into active producers and distributors. Whereas the democratization of information was once heralded as a phenomenal step towards greater equality, it has now become clear that the current phase of the internet is far less egalitarian, open and democratic than previously thought. Information comes to us through the secret algorithms of two major American companies. Facebook knows what we like and gives us more of what we like, allowing us to slowly drift off towards our snug filter bubbles where we can all talk with like-minded 'friends'. If people from the other side dare to talk to us, if they get angry at what we consider sacred, we call them 'trolls'. We have travelled quite some distance from the ideal of the *herrschaftsfreie Diskurs* (Jürgen Habermas) between citizens who might have differing views.

If Facebook raises invisible walls between us, Google fills both sides of the wall with unchecked content. The company considers itself a platform that discloses what is available on the internet, not an arbiter concerned with the veracity of information. Holocaust negationism thus becomes as valid as the second law of thermodynamics. As a result, 'fake news' (today's shorthand for what used to be called *lies*) has become a defining feature of life in a modern democracy, purposefully generated and circulated by political networks in order to distort public opinion and instil massive amounts of distrust towards traditional media which then can only be seen as *Lügenpresse*.[2]

One wall, two worlds. If the other side tries to talk to us, they can only be trolls. If we try to talk to them, we can only be from the *Lügenpresse*. And with these mindsets, we lace our shoes and walk to the voting booth.

Are you surprised the European Union is falling apart, Mr Juncker?

We urgently need to create spaces where citizens can come together, offline and online, despite their differences, to have access to reliable information in order to deliberate in an informed manner where society should be heading. And, frankly, we don't have these spaces any more. The public sphere has shrunk even further and our democracies are suffering from it. We use old procedures in entirely new contexts. We are travelling with eighteenth-century horse-carts amid the noise and the hooting of jammed-up twenty-first-century motorways.

By refusing to change procedures, we have made political turmoil and instability defining features of Western democracy. Brexit, Cameron's little ill-calculated electoral game, may cause a chain reaction with countries like France, the Netherlands and others deciding to hold EU referendums. It goes without saying that the exit of two founding members of the EU would constitute a fatal blow to the European dream, the largest peace-building effort history has ever witnessed.

Countless Western societies are currently afflicted by what we might call 'democratic fatigue syndrome'. Symptoms may include referendum fever, declining party membership and low voter turnout. Or government impotence and political paralysis – under relentless media scrutiny, widespread public distrust and populist upheavals. The World Values Survey paints a very grim portrait: fewer than half of young Europeans believe that living in a democracy is essential.[3] Yet democracy is not the problem. Voting is the problem.

This is the state of the European continent, Mr President. We are falling apart. Your State of the Union Address last September admitted that Europe was 'at least in part, in an existential crisis'.[4] But why then has the official reaction been so lame? Why don't we see a concerted, inspired effort to tackle this major crisis? Why don't we even see the beginning of a new and daring vision of what this Union could stand for?

I realize that the EU has always been better at slow procedures than quick answers. It is not a country, but a complex network of countries where diplomatic consensus does prevail over charismatic leadership. But we voted for you. Wasn't that the entire idea behind the 2014 election with its Spitzenkandidaten[5] and its televised debates on Euronews?

To give Europe a face? To make sure that the winning faction in the Parliament was going to preside over the Council? You won. Now you must lead.

Yet so far the EU has given Brexit the worst possible response: shrugging its shoulders and returning to the technical proceedings of the day. 'Well, the Leave campaign was based on so many lies, the EU need not engage in any introspection. Surely there won't be a chain reaction.'

So far you have also given the US election the worst possible response, by blaming Trump for his ignorance: 'I believe we will lose two years, until Mr Trump has toured the world that he doesn't know.' While this may be true, bluntly dismissing the likes of Trump, Farage and Johnson as nitwits and liars, while refusing to take the anger and the fear of so many voters behind them seriously, is only adding fuel to the fire. Yes, part of that anger may be imagined and inflated by populist rhetoric, but part of it is real and deserves your fullest attention.

If democracy has become a battle between trolls and liars, the European Union has increasingly become a battle between citizens and companies. What was once a pacifist project to bring national industries together in order to avoid new armed conflict is now a source of growing tension between private corporations and angry citizens.

There are again two Europes now; there are even once again two Germanys. And this time it is not East–West, or capitalist–communist. It is a divide between those who feel politically represented and those who don't – until the populist leader comes along. For at that moment, all the old resentments find an outlet in the new leader.

Martin Schulz, the current president of the European Parliament and former Spitzenkandidat for the socialists, recently even dared to call for an 'Aufstand der Anständigen', a revolt of the decent, thereby stigmatizing and demonizing large parts of the other Europe as 'indecent', in the same incredibly stupid way that Hillary Clinton described large swathes of Trump's electorate as 'a basket of deplorables'. Strange, for I was still under the impression that social democracy was about caring for the underprivileged.

For Guy Verhofstadt, your liberal challenger as Spitzenkandidat, the answer to Trump is not more democracy in

Europe, but more defence. As if the biggest danger does not come from within! The biggest threat to the EU these days is not Russia, but the EU itself. Herman Van Rompuy, however, the former president of the European Council, recently said: 'I always have to laugh when people start talking about the democratic deficit. I admit that the EU has to function better, but there is nothing wrong with its democratic quality.'

Whence this sense of superiority, Mr Juncker? Could it be something to do with your generation of political leaders? Could it be that you just don't see it? Because, regardless of your ideological differences, you all seem to agree that people have still not quite understood how good Europe is for them. 'Peace and prosperity', you all happily repeat, 'for the past seventy years'. But does this mantra still work for those confronted with the violence of globalization and the injustices of the world economic system that Europe has expedited? Can you actually imagine the violence of this age? Farmers and factory workers are losing their jobs because of globalization, soon middle-class employees will lose their jobs because of automatization. The future looks uncertain for ever more Europeans, and scapegoats are easily found. Muslims are easier to blame than robots.

You know why a certain phase of the European project is over? Because in the past the European Union has always been based on consensus, a consensus that was obtained among the ruling elites who imposed it upon the voting masses. But democracy is not so much about consensus as it is about conflict. And it is not even about solving conflicts, but about learning how to live with them. Democracy tries to handle conflicts before they turn into violence. So, at its very root, democracy is the celebration of conflict – but we have seen very little of that at the EU level. European laws have always more resembled gentlemen's agreements than compromises painstakingly fought over by the populace.

The main reason why the EU is falling apart is the perceived gap between its citizens and Brussels. It's time for citizens to have their say on Europe, not just through representation but through participation. Ticking a box every five years is not enough. Where is the reasoned voice of the people in all this? Where do European citizens get the chance to obtain the best possible information, engage with each other and decide collectively upon their future? Where do citizens get a chance to shape the fate of their communities? Not in the voting booth, for sure.

We should return to the central principle of Athenian democracy: drafting by lot, or sortition as it is presently called. In ancient Athens, the majority of public functions were assigned by lot. Renaissance states such as Venice and Florence worked on the same basis and experienced centuries of political stability. With sortition, you do not ask everyone to vote on an issue few people really understand, but you draft a random sample of the population and make sure they get to grips with the subject matter in order to be able to make a sensible decision. An informed cross section of society can act more coherently than an entire society that is uninformed.

Come on, take Europeans seriously. Let them speak. Why educate the masses if they are still not allowed to talk? Look at Ireland, the most innovative democracy in Europe. A few weeks ago, a random sample of one hundred Irish citizens, drafted by lot, was brought together into a Citizens' Assembly. This is a country that trusts its citizens instead of fearing them. Over the next year, they will discuss five topics, including abortion, referendums and climate change. They will invite all the experts they want to hear. This Assembly is the second of its kind: from 2012 to 2014, a similar procedure asked Irish citizens to make policy recommendations about a range of topics including marriage equality. Their proposal for constitutional reform was later voted on in a national referendum. It was the first time in modern history that a constitution was altered after deliberation by a random sample of citizens. Now, these are ways of doing democracy in the twenty-first century.

What if you called for a similar Citizens' Assembly in the European Union? Every European member state could bring together a random sample of one hundred citizens for four days, in order to answer one big question: *How do we make the European Union more democratic before 2020?* From Portugal to Estonia, participants would get the same amount of time and materials. Every country would formulate ten recommendations. After three months, twenty delegates from each national convention, again drafted by lot, would come together in Brussels to finalize the list of twenty-five shared priorities for future policy.

It would even be possible to subject this list to public scrutiny in the form of a referendum. But such a referendum would by no means take the shape of a traditional YES/NO question, but that of a *multiple-choice referendum*. The ballot would list all twenty-five propositions and give voters the chance to highlight the three topics which they deem most important. Alternatively, they could be asked to rate every single proposition on a scale from 1 to 5.

Multiple-choice referendums combine the best of elections with the best of traditional referendums: like a YES/NO referendum, they are about substantial content (and not just names); like elections, voters get a range of options to choose from (and not just one).

EU policy makers would get both results as sources of inspiration: the list of twenty-five priorities as drafted by the citizens' panel, as well as the outcome of the multiple-choice referendum.

Combining citizens' panels drafted by lot with multiple-choice referendums open to anyone is a great way to improve democracy: it includes citizens in the decision-making process, it celebrates informed opinion over gut feeling, and it unites rather than divides societies.

This would constitute some real change. By letting citizens speak, you would create an agenda for future action that was generated from the bottom up. You would give citizens an active role in shaping their Europe. You would open up an innovative path between those calling for 'more Europe' and those who 'want their country back'. You would create a new dynamic between member states and Brussels. And more importantly, you would bring the two Europes together in real dialogue, rather than digital diatribe.

In your State of the Union Address, President Juncker, you rightly said that the 'next twelve months are the crucial time to deliver a better Europe'. You even called for a 'Europe that empowers'. Sadly, this went no further than promising 5G internet and a voluntary corps. With 5G, we will get even faster into our filter bubbles where fake news reigns. With a corps consisting of volunteers, there is little chance that a German Neo-Nazi, a refugee from Syria and an urban hipster will rub shoulders. How dare you come up with such weak solutions at the moment the EU is agonizing? Today's challenge is of an entirely different magnitude: re-establishing trust in a unique project by involving citizens in the debate about the future of their communities. Democracy is government of the people not only for the people, but also by the people. We have less than a year.

Notes

1 See Bernard Manin, *Kritik der repräsentativen Demokratie*, Berlin: Matthes & Seitz, 2007.
2 A pejorative term the German right (Pegida, AfD) uses for mainstream media.
3 See Roberto Stefan Foa and Yascha Mounk, 'The Democratic Discontent', *Journal of Democracy*, 27:3 (2016), p. 7, at http://www.journalofdemocracy.org/sites/default/files/Foa%26Mounk-27-3.pdf (retrieved January 2017).
4 Jean-Claude Juncker, 'State of the Union Address 2016: Towards a Better Europe – a Europe that Protects, Empowers and Defends', 14 September 2016, at http://ec.europa.eu/priorities/state-union-2016_en (retrieved January 2017).
5 The German term for leading candidates for the Presidency of the European Commission.

15

The populist temptation

Slavoj Žižek

There are two faulty generalizations about today's society currently circulating. The first is that we live in an era of universalized anti-Semitism: with the military defeat of fascism, the role once played by the anti-Semitic figure of the Jew is now played by any foreign group experienced as a threat to our identity – Latinos, Africans, and especially Muslims, who are today in Western society increasingly treated as the new 'Jew'. The other generalization is that the fall of the Berlin Wall has led to the proliferation of new walls intended to separate us from the dangerous Other (the wall separating Israel from the West Bank, the planned wall between the US and Mexico, etc.) – true enough, except that there is a key difference between the two kinds of wall. The Berlin Wall stood for the Cold War division of the world, and although it was perceived as the barrier that kept the populations of the 'totalitarian' communist states isolated, it also signalled that capitalism was not the only option, that an alternative to it, although a failed one, existed. By contrast, the walls that we see rising today, though their construction was triggered by the fall of the Berlin Wall (i.e., the disintegration of the communist order), don't stand for the division between capitalism and communism but for a division that is strictly immanent to the global capitalist order. In a nice Hegelian move, when capitalism won over its external enemy and united the world, the division returned in its own space.

As for the first generalization, there is a rather obvious distinction between fascism proper and today's anti-immigrant populism.[1] Let's recall the basic premise of the Marxist analysis of capitalism: capitalism is a reign of abstraction; in it, social relations are permeated, regulated and dominated by abstractions which are not just subjective abstractions performed by our minds, but 'objective' abstractions, abstractions that rule social reality itself, what Marx called *Realabstraktion*. These abstractions are part of our social experience in capitalism: we directly experience our social life as regulated by impenetrable mechanisms that are beyond representation, that cannot be embodied in any individual – even the capitalists who replaced the old Masters are enslaved by powers beyond their control. No wonder that, today, ideological *prosopopoeia* is having a heyday: the markets have started to talk again as living persons, expressing their 'worry' at what will happen if the elections fail to produce a government with a mandate to continue with the programme of fiscal austerity.

The anti-Semitic figure of the 'Jew' embodies this abstraction, as the invisible Master who secretly pulls the strings. Since Jews are fully integrated into our society, posing deceivingly as one of us, the problem and task is to clearly identify them (recall all the ridiculous Nazi attempts to measure precise racial identities). Muslim immigrants are *not* today's Jews: they are all too visible, clearly not integrated into our societies, and nobody claims that they are secretly pulling the strings. If one suspects a secret plot in their 'invasion of Europe', then Jews have to be behind it, as recently proposed in a text that appeared in one of the main Slovene rightist weekly journals where we could read: 'George Soros is one of the most depraved and dangerous people of our time, responsible for the invasion of the negroid and Semitic hordes and thereby for the twilight of the EU ... as a typical Talmudo-Zionist, he is a deadly enemy of the Western civilization, nation-state and white, European man.' His goal, the author continues, is to build a 'rainbow coalition composed of social marginals like faggots, feminists, Muslims and work-hating cultural Marxists' which would then perform 'a deconstruction of the nation-state, and transform the EU into a multicultural dystopia of the United States of Europe'. So which forces are opposing Soros? 'Viktor Orbán and Vladimir Putin are the perspicuous politicians who have wholly grasped Soros's machinations and, logically, prohibited the activity of his organizations.' Furthermore, according to the Slovene commentator, Soros is inconsistent in his promotion of multiculturalism:

> He promotes it exclusively in Europe and the USA, while in the case of Israel he, in a way which is for me totally justified, agrees with its monoculturalism, latent racism and building a wall. In contrast to the EU and USA, he also does not demand of Israel that it open its borders and accept 'refugees'. A hypocrisy proper to Talmudo-Zionism.[2]

Apart from the stunning racist directness of this text, one should note two features. First, it brings together anti-Semitism and Islamophobia: the threat to Europe comes from hordes of Muslim refugees, but behind this chaotic phenomenon are the Jews. Second, it clearly takes side in the conflict within the European right with regard to Putin: on the one hand, Putin is a threat to Europe, especially to the neighbouring post-communist countries, and is trying to undermine the EU with his machinations; on the other hand, he saw the danger of Western multiculturalism and permissiveness and wisely prevented his country from being overwhelmed by it.

Only against this background can we grasp Trump's inconsistent stance towards Russia: while hard-line Republicans continuously attacked Obama for his all-too-soft stance towards Putin, tolerating Russian military aggression (Georgia, Crimea ...) and thereby endangering Western allies in Eastern Europe, Trump supporters now advocate a much more lenient approach to Russia. The underlying problem is this: how are we to unite the opposition of traditionalism versus secular relativism with the other big ideological opposition on which the entire legitimacy of the West and its 'war on terror' relies, namely that between liberal-democratic individual rights and the religious fundamentalism embodied primarily in 'Islamo-fascism'? Therein lies the symptomatic inconsistency of the US neoconservatives: while in domestic politics they privilege the fight against liberal secularism (abortion, gay marriage, etc.), pitting the so-called 'culture of life' against the 'culture of death', in foreign policy they privilege the opposite values of the liberal 'culture of death'.

At some deep and often obfuscated level, the neocons see the European Union as *the* enemy. This perception, kept under wraps in the public political discourse, explodes in its underground obscene double, the extreme-right Christian fundamentalist political vision, with its obsessive fear of a New World Order (Obama was in secret collusion with the United Nations to enable international forces to intervene in the US and put all true American patriots in concentration camps – a couple of years ago, there were rumours that Latino-American troops were already in the Midwest building the camps ...). One way to resolve this dilemma is the hard-line Christian fundamentalist one, articulated in the works of Tim LaHaye and others: to unambiguously subordinate the second opposition to the first. The title of one of LaHaye's novels points in this direction: *The Europa Conspiracy*. The true enemy of the US is not the Muslim terrorists, since they are merely puppets secretly manipulated by the true forces of the Antichrist, namely the European secularists who want to weaken the US and establish the New World Order under the domination of the United Nations. In a way, they are right: Europe is not just another geopolitical power bloc, but represents a global vision that is ultimately incompatible with the continued existence of nation-states. This dimension of the EU provides the key to the so-called European 'weakness': there is a surprising correlation between European unification and Europe's loss of global military-political power. But if the EU is an increasingly impotent trans-state confederacy in need of American protection, why then is the United States ill at ease with it? Recall the indications that the US financially supported those forces in Ireland organizing the campaign for saying NO to the new European treaty ...

Opposed to this minority view is the predominant liberal-democratic view that sees the principal enemy in all kinds of fundamentalisms, and perceives US Christian fundamentalism as a deplorable home-grown version of 'Islamo-fascism'. This predominance, however, is now under threat: what was until recently a marginal opinion limited to conspiracy theorists inhabiting the underground of social media is becoming a hegemonic view in our public space. Both Trump and Putin supported Brexit, they both take the extreme conservative-nationalist line of 'America/Russia first' which sees a united Europe as its biggest enemy – and they are both right. Europe's problem is how to remain faithful to its legacy, threatened as it now is by the conservative-populist onslaught. The first thing to do in order to redeem that legacy is to probe into the deeper causes of Trump's success. Trump is a perfect example of the Two-Spirit Capitalist whose formula was already provided in *Citizen Kane*. When Kane is attacked by Thatcher, a representative of big banking capital, for using his money to finance a newspaper that speaks for the underprivileged, Kane replies:

> The trouble is, you don't realize you're talking to two people. As Charles Foster Kane, who owns eighty-two thousand, three hundred and sixty-four shares of Metropolitan Transfer – you see, I do have a rough idea of my holdings – I sympathize with you. Charles Foster Kane is a scoundrel, his paper should be run out of town, a committee should be formed to boycott him. You may, if you can form such a committee, put me down for a contribution of one thousand dollars … On the other hand, I am the publisher of the *Enquirer*. As such, it is my duty – and I'll let you in on a little secret, it is also my pleasure – to see to it that the decent, hard-working people of this city aren't robbed blind by a pack of money-mad pirates just because, God help them, they have no one to look after their interests! I'll let you in on another little secret, Mr. Thatcher. I think I'm the man to do it. You see, I have money and property. If I don't defend the interests of the underprivileged, maybe somebody else will – maybe somebody without any money or property, and that would be too bad.[3]

The last sentence gives the succinct formula for what is wrong with the billionaire Trump posing as the voice of the dispossessed: his strategic function is to prevent them from defending themselves. Trump is thus far from being simply inconsistent; what appears as inconsistency is the very core of his project.

Echoing this inconsistency are two reactions to the Trump victory that should both be rejected as unacceptable and

ultimately self-destructive. The first is the arrogant fasci-
nation with the stupidity of ordinary voters who fell for
Trump's superficial demagoguery and just didn't get that
they were voting against their own interests. The second
is the call for an immediate counter-offensive – 'No time
to philosophize, we have to act!' – which strangely echoes
Trump's own anti-intellectual stance. (Judith Butler has per-
spicuously noted that, as is the case with every populist
demagogue, Trump is giving the people 'an occasion not to
think, an occasion not to have to think. To think is to think
of a very complex global world, and he's making everything very, very simple.'⁴ Of course, as Butler is fully aware,
while Clinton presented herself as someone well versed in
the complexities of real politics, her reference to 'complexity' was no less false since it was also used to defuse leftist
demands.)

The first reaction is a complaint about how the popular
rage exploited by figures like Trump and anti-immigrant populists in Europe entails a 'regression of political culture' – a
regression into demagogic vulgarities that, even a couple of
years ago, would not have been tolerated in public space but
that have now become a commonplace, presenting a 'clear
and present danger' to our democracy. The second no less
deplorable reaction is a variation on the old theme 'if you
can't beat them, join them!': from Greece to France, a new
trend is arising in what remains of the 'radical left' – the
rediscovery of nationalism. The idea is that, in the popular
rage that engulfs us, the people have woken up, making their
discontent clear, and what the dominant media denounce
as a dangerous turn is in fact the forceful return of class
struggle. The task of the left is thus to reject the liberal
fear and assume this rage, channelling it away from rightist
racism into direct socioeconomic struggle: the enemy is not
the foreigner but the ruling class, the financial oligarchy, etc.
From this standpoint, the movements identified by the names
'Trump' and 'Sanders' represent two forms of populism, both
reintroducing an antagonistic anti-establishment passion into
politics. (It is of course absurd to consider Trump, a billionaire exploiting all the legal loopholes, 'anti-establishment' in
any meaningful sense, but this is the paradox of populism
from the very beginning.)

Each of the two positions has a point: good manners should never be underestimated in politics, and a vulgar public speech by definition indicates a deeper political disorientation; it is also true that the rightist populist rage is a distorted form of class struggle, as was already the case in fascism. However, both positions are also fundamentally flawed. Liberal critics of the new populism fail to see that the popular anger is a sign not of the primitivism of ordinary people but of the weakness of the hegemonic liberal ideology itself, which, since it can no longer 'manufacture consent', must have recourse to a more 'primitive' functioning of ideology instead. The leftist advocates of populism fail to see that 'populism' is not a neutral form that can be given either a rightist-fascist or a leftist spin. Already at the level of its form, populism constructs the enemy as an external intruder and thereby denies immanent social antagonisms.[5] For this reason, while populism in no way necessarily entails the disintegration of public discourse into vulgarity, it nonetheless clearly manifests something like a natural propensity to slide into vulgar simplification and personalized aggressiveness.

The populist left accepts all too quickly the basic premise of its enemy: universalism is out, dismissed as the lifeless political and cultural counterpart of 'rootless' global capital and its technocratic financial experts, or at best as the ideology of Habermasian social democrats advocating global capitalism with a human face. The reason for this rediscovery of nationalism is obvious: the rise of rightist nationalist populism in Western Europe, which is now the strongest political force advocating the protection of working-class interests, and simultaneously the strongest political force able to give rise to proper political passions. Why then should the left leave this field of nationalist passions to the radical right, why should it not 'reclaim *la patrie* from the Front National'? Could the radical left not mobilize these same nationalist passions as a mighty weapon against the dominant force in today's global society, the increasingly unfettered reign of rootless financial capital? Once we accept this horizon, the very fact that the critique of the Brussels technocracy from the standpoint of national sovereignty curtailed by anonymous bureaucrats is the main feature of today's radical right becomes a reason for leftist patriotism. In Greece, this is the opposition between Varoufakis and Lapavitsas, who mocks the former's DIEM initiative for its lifeless pan-Europeanism which accepts in advance the enemy's terrain.

The main theoretical proponent of leftist populism is Chantal Mouffe.[6] According to her diagnosis of our predicament, the main reason for the failure of the left is its non-combative stance of rational argumentation and lifeless universalism, epitomized by the names of Giddens, Beck and Habermas, which brought an end to the old passionate ideological struggles. Since this post-political Third Way is no match for the agonistic logic of Us against Them successfully mobilized by anti-immigrant populists like Marine Le Pen, the only way to combat such rightist populism is by recourse to a leftist populism which, while retaining the basic populist coordinates and agonistic logic, fills them in with leftist content: 'They' are no longer the poor refugees and immigrants but the financial capitalists, the technocratic state bureaucracy, etc. This leftist populism also moves beyond the old working-class anti-capitalism, bringing together a multiplicity of struggles from ecology to feminism, from the right to employment to the right to free education and healthcare, etc., as Podemos is doing in Spain. But is such a formula of agonistic politicization, of passionate confrontation as opposed to lifeless universalism, not precisely all too formal? Does it not ignore the big question that lurks in the background: Why did the left abandon the agonistic logic of Us versus Them in the first place?

It is absolutely crucial to take note of a feature shared by the politically correct respect for particular identities and the anti-immigrant hatred of others: the fear that a particular identity will be swallowed up in the nameless universality of a global New World Order. When conservative nationalists point out that they just want for their own nation (for the Germans, French, British ...) the same right to identity that sexual and ethnic minorities want for themselves, this utterly hypocritical demand nonetheless makes a valid point; namely, that we need to move beyond *all* forms of identity politics, rightist and leftist. What one should reject is, already at a more basic level, the perspective of multiple local struggles for emancipation (ethnic, sexual, religious, legal ...) which should then gradually be united by way of building an always fragile 'chain of equivalences' between them (to use Ernesto Laclau's expression). Universality is not something that should emerge through a long and patient process, it is something that is always already here as the starting point of every authentic emancipatory process, as its very motivation.

Formally, then, the problem is how to combine the two axes: universality versus patriotic belonging and capitalism versus leftist anti-capitalism. All four possible combinations are occupied: we have global multicultural capitalism, we have a universalist left, we have an anti-globalist patriotic left, and we have capitalism with local ethnic/cultural 'character-istics' (China, India ...). This last combination is becoming stronger and stronger, proving that global capitalism can ideally coexist with particular cultural identities. Plus we should always bear in mind the properly Hegelian paradox of today's universal class of managers and elite academics. Within each particular community (nation), this elite appears as a particular group isolated from the majority by their whole lifestyle: a humanities professor in New York has much more in common with a humanities professor in Paris or even Seoul than with a worker who lives on Staten Island. The form of appearance of a universal class which reaches across particular nations is as an extreme particularity within its nation – universality divides a particular identity from within.

That's why we have to shift our focus from the Big Bad Wolf of populism to the true problem: the weakness of the moderate 'rational' position itself. The fact that the majority are unconvinced by 'rational' capitalist propaganda and are much more prone to endorse a populist, anti-elitist stance is not to be discounted as a case of lower-class primitivism: populists correctly detect the irrationality of this rationalism, and their rage directed at the faceless institutions that regu-late their lives in a non-transparent way is fully justified. The lesson to be learned from the Trump phenomenon is that the greatest danger for the true left would be to accept a strategic pact with Clintonite liberals against the Big Danger embodied in Trump. And this lesson has a long-term relevance, since the story of Donald and Hillary goes on: in its second instalment, the couple's names change into Marine Le Pen and Fran-çois Fillon. Now that Fillon has been elected as the right's candidate in the forthcoming French presidential elections,

and with the near certainty that the choice in the second
round will be between Fillon and Le Pen, our democracy has
reached its (till now) lowest point. As Natalie Nougayrède
wrote in her *Guardian* column, 'François Fillon is as big a
threat to liberal values as Marine Le Pen':

> It is no coincidence that Fillon was publicly lauded by Putin.
> This wasn't just because the Kremlin hopes to find a French
> presidential ally on foreign policy. It's also because Putin
> detects in Fillon streaks of his own ultra-conservative ideol-
> ogy. According to this world-view, liberal progressive values
> have brought western societies to a state of 'decadence', as
> a result of sexual policies and immigration. Witness how
> Russian propaganda has dubbed Europe 'Gayropa'.[7]

If in the case of Clinton and Trump the difference was
between the liberal establishment and rightist populist rage,
this shrinks to a minimum in the case of Le Pen versus Fillon.
While both are cultural conservatives, in matters of economy
Fillon is purely neoliberal while Le Pen is much more oriented
towards protecting workers' interests. Fillon represents the
worst combination around today – economic neoliberalism
and social conservativism; the only argument for Fillon is a
purely formal one: he *formally* stands for a united Europe
and a minimal distance from the populist right.

In this sense, Fillon stands for the immanent decadence
of the establishment itself – here is where we have ended
up after a long series of defeats and withdrawals. First, the
radical left had to be sacrificed for being out of touch with
our new postmodern times and 'paradigms'. Then the moderate social-democratic left had to be sacrificed as also being
out of touch with the necessities of the new global capitalism.
Now, in the final chapter of this sad tale, the moderate liberal
right itself (Juppé) has been sacrificed for being out of touch
with the conservative values which have to be enlisted if we,
the civilized world, want to beat Le Pen. Any resemblance
to the old story of how the Nazis in power came first for the
communists, then the Jews, then the moderate left, then the
liberal centre, then even honest conservatives ... is purely
accidental. In such a situation, to abstain from voting is obviously the *only* appropriate thing to do.

Today's liberal left and populist right are both caught in the politics of fear: fear of immigrants, of feminists, etc., or the fear of fundamentalist populists, etc. The first thing to do here is to accomplish the move from fear to *Angst*: fear is the fear of an external object that is perceived as posing a threat to our identity, while anxiety emerges when we become aware that there is something wrong with our identity which we want to protect from the feared external threat. Fear pushes us to annihilate the external object, while the way to confront anxiety is to transform ourselves. One is tempted to turn around Gramsci's famous statement about the 'morbid symptoms' that arise when the old order is dying and the new order is not yet born: when an order rules, horrors and monstrosities are normalized; but in the process of passage from the old to the new, the horrors become visible as such, become de-normalized – and in such moments of hope, great acts become possible.

The urgency of the present situation should in no way serve as an excuse – the urgent situation *is* the time to think. We should also not be afraid here to turn around Marx's Thesis XI: until now we have tried to change our world too quickly; the time has come to reinterpret it self-critically, examining our own (leftist) responsibility. And this is what we should do today when we are under the spell of Trump's victory (which, let us not forget, is just one in a series of similar bad surprises): we need to reject both defeatism and blind activism and 'learn, learn, and learn' (as Lenin would have put it) what has caused this fiasco of liberal-democratic politics. In his *Notes Towards the Definition of Culture*,[8] the great conservative T. S. Eliot remarked that there are moments when the only choice is that between heresy and non-belief, when the only way to keep a religion alive is to effect a sectarian split from its main corpse. This is what has to be done today: the US elections of 2016 were the final blow to the Fukuyama dream, the final defeat of liberal democracy, and the only way to really overcome Trump and redeem what is worth saving in liberal democracy is to effect a sectarian split from liberal democracy's main corpse. In short, to shift the weight from Clinton to Sanders – the next election should be between Trump and Sanders.

Elements of the programme for this new left are relatively easy to imagine. Obviously, the only way to counteract the

'democratic deficit' of global capitalism would have been
through some transnational entity – was it not already Kant,
more than two hundred years ago, who saw the need for
a trans-nation-state legal order grounded in the rise of a
global society? 'Since the narrower or wider community of
the peoples of the earth has developed so far that a violation
of rights in one place is felt throughout the world, the idea
of a law of world citizenship is no high-flown or exagger-
ated notion.'[9] This, however, brings us to what is arguably
the 'principal contradiction' of the New World Order: the
structural impossibility of creating a global political order
which would correspond to the global capitalist economy.
What if, for structural reasons and due not only to empirical limitations, there can be no worldwide democracy or
representative world government? The antinomy of global
capitalism resides in the impossibility (and, simultaneously,
necessity) of a sociopolitical order that would fit it: the global
market economy cannot be directly organized as a global
liberal democracy with worldwide elections. In politics, the
'repressed' of the global economy returns in archaic fixations
and particular substantial identities (ethnic, religious, cultural). This tension defines our predicament today: the global
free circulation of commodities is accompanied by growing
divisions in the social sphere – while commodities circulate
more and more freely, more and more people are kept apart
by new walls.

Trump promises the cancellation of the major free trade
agreements supported by Clinton; the left alternative should
be a programme of new and different international agreements – agreements which would establish control of the
banks, enforce ecological standards, secure workers' rights,
healthcare services, the protection of sexual and ethnic
minorities, etc. The big lesson of global capitalism is that
nation-states acting alone cannot do the job – only a new
political international can possibly bridle global capital.
An old anti-communist leftist once told me that the only
good thing about Stalin was that he really scared the big
Western powers, and one could say the same about Trump:
the only good thing about him is that he really scares liberals.
The Western powers learned their lesson and self-critically
focused on their own shortcomings, developing the welfare

state – will our left liberals be willing or able to do something similar?

Trump's victory has created a totally new political situation, with opportunities for a more radical political left. Now is the time for the hard work of forming that left. Or, to quote Mao: 'There is disorder under heaven; the situation is excellent.'

Notes

1 I rely here on Alenka Zupančič, 'AIMO', *Mladina* (Winter 2016/2017) (in Slovene).

2 Quoted from Bernard Brščič, 'George Soros is One of the Most Depraved and Dangerous People of our Time', *Demokracija*, 25 August 2016, p. 15 (in Slovene).

3 Quoted from http://www.dailyscript.com/scripts/citizenkane. html.

4 Scott MacLeod, 'Global Trouble: American philosopher Judith Butler Discusses American Vulgarity, Middle East Upheaval, and Other Forms of the Global Crisis', *The Cairo Review of Global Affairs* (Fall 2016), at https://www.thecairoreview.com/q-a/global-trouble (retrieved December 2016).

5 For a conceptual critique of the leftist use of populism, see Chapter 6 of Slavoj Žižek, *In Defense of Lost Causes*, London and New York: Verso, 2009.

6 For a short presentation of her position, see Chantal Mouffe, 'Pour un populisme de gauche', *Le Monde*, 21 April 2016, p. 22.

7 Natalie Nougayrède, 'François Fillon is as Big a Threat to Liberal Values as Marine Le Pen', *Guardian*, 28 November 2016, at https://www.theguardian.com/commentisfree/2016/nov/28/francois-fillon-threat-liberal-values-marine-le-pen-france (retrieved December 2016).

8 See T. S. Eliot, *Notes Towards the Definition of Culture*, London: Faber & Faber, 1973.

9 Immanuel Kant, *Perpetual Peace*, ed. Lewis White Beck, Indianapolis: Bobbs-Merrill, 1957, p. 23.